Organizational Values and Political Power:
The Forest Service Versus the Olympic National Park

*The Pennsylvania State
University Studies No. 48*

Organizational Values and Political Power:

The Forest Service Versus the Olympic National Park

by Ben W. Twight

The Pennsylvania State University Press
University Park and London

Cover photograph courtesy of the National Park Service

Library of Congress Cataloging in Publication Data

Twight, Ben W., 1933–

Organizational values and political power.

(The Pennsylvania State University studies; no. 48)
1. United States. Forest Service—History.
2. Olympic National Park (Wash.)—History.   3. Forest
policy—United States—History.   4. United States.
National Park Service—History.   I. Title.   II. Series.
SD565.T84   1983   353.0082'338   83-4103
ISBN 0-271-00353-7

12.4.85 AC

Copyright © 1983 The Pennsylvania State University

Designed by Dolly Carr

Printed in the United States of America

Contents

Part 2 The Case Study

Part 3 An Interpretation

Preface

This is a study of how tenacious adherence to a system of values by a professional bureaucracy, the United States Forest Service, guided that agency's political decisions over a twenty-nine-year period to the ultimate loss of jurisdiction over almost a million acres of public forest. Not only are agency values and their influence on organizational decisions demonstrated, but also the militance of professional bureaus in their attempts to influence legislation. The study is also a history of the contest for power between two federal agencies and their clientele groups over Washington State's Olympic Mountains, developed from the perspective of the incumbent agency. This history is different in that it illustrates that perspective from both high and low levels of the Forest Service as the organization jealously defends its domain through efforts to dominate the social environment. Contrary to other studies which advance the external control of bureaucracy view, this study documents how a bureau was impelled to achieve its internal vision of order, despite strong external influences. Both the external pressures for organizational change and the internal commitment to the American forester's traditional values and premises are depicted, based on hundreds of letters and documents from the official archives of the Forest Service.

The first chapter provides a general overview of the history of the conservation of public forest lands in the United States, both for aesthetic and economic purposes. Chapter 2 describes the concept of value orientation as it affects the decision-making frame of reference in forestry; this section includes an analysis of the origins of the federal forester's values and of how those values are socialized into the members of the bureaucracy. The historical analysis of the case of the Olympic Mountains is broken into three chapters covering the period from 1909, when President Theodore Roosevelt established the Mount Olympus National Monument under the jurisdiction of the U.S. Forest Service, to 1938, when President Franklin D. Roosevelt signed a bill establishing the monument and surrounding Forest Service lands as the

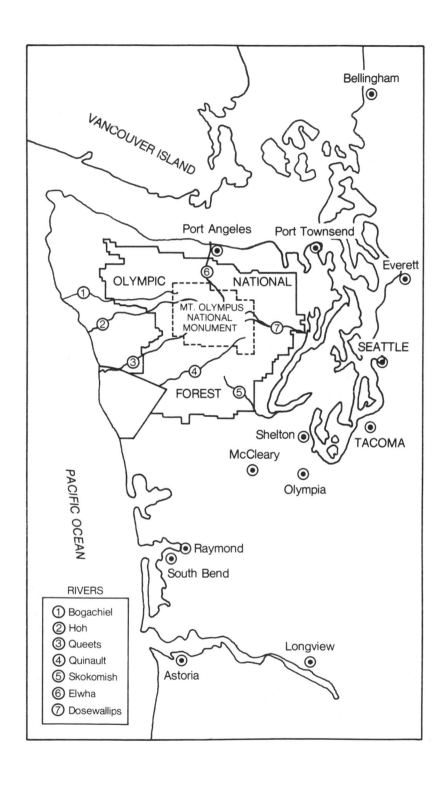

Bellingham

VANCOUVER ISLAND

Port Angeles   Port Townsend

Everett

OLYMPIC   NATIONAL

MT. OLYMPUS
NATIONAL
MONUMENT

SEATTLE

FOREST

Shelton   TACOMA

McCleary

Olympia

PACIFIC OCEAN

Raymond

South Bend

Longview

Astoria

RIVERS

① Bogachiel
② Hoh
③ Queets
④ Quinault
⑤ Skokomish
⑥ Elwha
⑦ Dosewallips

Olympic National Park. Throughout this analysis the values and premises of the foresters are illustrated by their rhetoric and are identified or summarized as the case proceeds; the values of the agency's opponents are also evidenced here from time to time. The reader is advised to carefully note these values and premises in the second chapter, so that their use will be more obvious when they appear later in the dialectic of the foresters.

The final chapter discusses the outcome of the case in relation to the two alternative hypotheses, that of accommodation of the external forces in the organization's environment versus that of internal direction by value orientation, and thus the effort to dominate the environment. Comparisons with similar cases in the same and other agencies are made; an analogy of the outcome to Talcott Parson's fiduciary model of power completes the study.[1] A discussion of value theory is included in the appendix.

This study is not intended to show the "good guys" against the "bad guys"; it is a look at the conflicting values that have been and continue to be held by honorable men of both conservation persuasions. Readers who hold aesthetic convictions should remember that there can be little appreciation of those values of forests without first acquiring the prosperity to afford that appreciation. It is also important to note that the foresters were not power-hungry villains; these professionals attempted to mobilize power because they sincerely believed they were *right*, and thus attempts to dominate the social environment were quite natural.

It may also be true that the agency was merely loyally defending its professional function; however, Max Weber once observed that behind the functional purposes of a bureaucracy "ideas of culture values usually stand."[2] Thus, it is not unreasonable to assume that an ideologically hallowed system of values and premises came to form the frame of reference of the foresters.

In this case, the members of the U.S. Forest Service realized that *power*—the probability that one can carry out his or her will in a social relationship in spite of resistance—ultimately determines whose values will prevail.[3] Though they struggled to retain control, power itself was not the most important goal of the foresters. Their value orientation was ultimately more important. When the field staff found that their beliefs about the proper use of the forest were to be rejected in spite of their efforts, they suggested it would be better to lose rather than to compromise. And the forest became a national park.

I am grateful to many persons for their help in this study. Professors William R. Catton, Jr., and Fremont J. Lyden gave me my theoretical training and provided valuable advice for the final version of this monograph; Professor Grant W. Sharpe suggested the historical conflict with which to test the theory and made the opportunity to do the study possible; and the late Professor George A. Shipman gave the study coherence and encouraged the author whenever he foundered. Professor Samuel P. Hays and Dr. Harold K. Steen both provided incisive and helpful reviews of the manuscript.

In addition, editorial director John Pickering of The Pennsylvania State University Press furnished strong inspiration. My secretary, Connie Daye, rigorously applied her knowledge of style; and, far from least, my wife, Patricia, shared more than equally with me the tasks of editing, organizing, and polishing the manuscript.

My thanks to them all.

Part 1   The Setting

1

The National Forests: A History

Romantic Roots

The origins of public interest in and generation of demand for wildland recreation in the United States can be traced to a handful of urban Romantic writers and artists in the early nineteenth century. Only after the rise of urban centers of culture and affluence did the wildlands become places of refreshment, inspiration, and adventure, rather than obstacles to be overcome or enemies to be conquered.[1]

The Romantic writers, among them *New York Post* editor William Cullen Bryant, were most influential in the urban centers during the mid-1800s. Their articles on nature and country instilled tastes for wildlands, art, architecture, and landscape gardens in the minds of both the affluent and those who aspired to affluence. The appreciation of wild scenery was widely propagated in the urban centers by books and cultural magazines such as *Century, Harper's Weekly*, and *Atlantic Monthly*. Inspired by the Romantic landscapes of artists Thomas Cole, Asher Durand, and Frederic Church, landscape painters of the Hudson River School glorified the American wilderness on canvas, often bathing nature in a kind of supernatural light. Western artists Albert Bierstadt and Thomas Moran brought to the urban East the drama of Yosemite, Yellowstone, and the Grand Tetons, as did the landscape photography of William H. Jackson.[2]

As the cities grew, their cultural level also increased. Frederick Law Olmsted's landscape parks, efforts to bring the "unspoiled countryside" into the city, grew more and more popular among the upper classes, and reached their peak in popularity after the Chicago Columbian Exposition of 1893. Preservation of wildlands, or of urban sophisticates of them, was so widely appreciated in this country in the 1890s that historian Roderick Nash suggests that a virtual wilderness cult existed.[3]

Economic Roots

Nineteenth century sentiment over American wildlands was not confined to the Romanticists. While the original land policy of the United

States was one of disposal into private ownership, the "cut and move on" attitude that prevailed among the large timber entrepreneurs in the mid- to late 1800s began to raise spectres of depletion and natural resource

In 1864 George Perkins Marsh's *Man and Nature* aroused interest in the idea that western man historically had abused his power to modify natural resources. Marsh particularly emphasized the adverse economic effects of excessive removal of forests, such as those resulting from the recent movement of the New England timber industry from Maine, through Pennsylvania, to the Lake States, later to the South, and finally into northwestern United States. Marsh made the analogy between these exploitive actions and those of Mediterranean empires of the past, where entire forests were permanently decimated.[4]

The early scientific interest generated by Marsh led to governmental studies and inventories of the United States forest situation. Interest was further stimulated by an 1873 report by Franklin B. Hough to the American Association for the Advancement of Science, entitled "On the Duty of Governments in the Preservation of Forests." At Hough's suggestion, the AAAS resolved that "a committee be appointed by the association to memorialize Congress and the several state legislatures upon the importance of promoting the cultivation of timber and the preservation of forests, and to recommend proper legislation for securing these objects."[5] Hough was commissioned by the Department of Agriculture to study the forests in 1876, shortly after the formation of the American Forestry Association.

Two subsequent government studies added further impetus to the move for a change in the United States land disposal policy. These were John Wesley Powell's U.S. Geological Survey *Report on the Lands of the Arid Region of the U.S.* in 1879 and the *Report of the Public Land Commission,* made in 1880. The former was an ecologically sensitive call for scientific federal land planning in the West. The Public Land Commission report recommended that all United States public forest acreage be withdrawn from further sale, with the timber from each even-numbered survey section to be harvested and sold for cash, and the proceeds to help "in the maintenance and reproduction of the forest."[6] The current disposal system into private ownership, however, continued eleven more years, when the General Land Law Revision of 1891 provided presidential authority for establishment of the first national forest reserves.

Congress, still unsure of the best approach to the management of forest reserves, was beset by suggestions from urban preservationist groups, like the newly formed Sierra Club, on the one hand and by utilitarian economic organizations, such as the American Forestry Association and its secretary, German forester Bernhard Fernow, on the other. Both of these interests, later seconded by American forester Gifford Pinchot, maintained that the destruction of forests was hurting the welfare of the country. The argument that a timber famine was imminent was later extended by Pinchot to project the demise of other major industries. A concerned Congress passed further legislation in 1897 that provided for management of the reserves, timber sales, etc.[7]

At the same time, Congress appropriated an additional $175,000 for the Geological Survey to determine whether there was indeed a problem with the national timber supply. The report by Henry Gannett, who piloted the three-year study, noted that "in view of the agitation which has been going on for at least a generation, and which has reached such an intensity that it has become with many persons almost a religion, it is strange that there should be practically no knowledge to serve as a basis for such a cult." Gannett found the timber resources of the nation still abundant, and predicted that better private management of forest resources would logically follow in time with diminishing supplies and associated price increases. Political scientist Norman Wengert observes:

> Gannett was much less fearful than many who would very soon be deeply involved in the conservation movement, and his comprehensive and long-range point of view set him off from the more ardent conservationists who were to influence public policy in a variety of ways in the next several decades. Had his report received more attention and his premises found their way into action, the history of American forestry would probably have been much different.[8]

The combined fervor of the preservationists and utilitarian conservationists prevailed; and the ongoing program of national forest reservations climaxed during the progressive conservation movement in the early 1900s under Pinchot and President Theodore Roosevelt.

The Uneasy Partnership

A split between the conservationists and the preservationists soon occurred. Historian Samuel P. Hays documented its development, showing that it had been a marriage of convenience between them and that the moral tone of *utilitarian* conservation was actually a rhetorical cover for the first efforts at centralized state planning in this country. The real implications of the utilitarian conservationists' campaign against the waste of natural resources were to be found in their belief in the application of science to government. Calling for long-term *planning* of all natural resources in the public interest, the progressive utilitarians felt that resource decisions should be scientifically made by government experts, uncontaminated by personal, aesthetic, or profit-oriented values. Their "gospel of efficiency," as Hays calls it, subordinated aesthetic values and discounted any persons who were concerned with nature preservation.

Interest in wilderness preservation, on the other hand, continued to grow in the final decade of the 1800s. The passage of the Yosemite National Park Act of 1890 and the New York Adirondack State Park Act of 1892 indicated current substantial political support for wildland reservations on both coasts. The campaign of William Gladstone Steel and the Portland (Oregon) Alpine Club, from 1886 on, resulted in the creation of the Cascade Forest Reserve under the 1891 Forest Reserve Act, lending further evidence of the extent of recreationist political influence. James Gilligan notes that a "great movement concerning lands originally primeval wilderness but containing . . . unique . . . scenery was well established . . . before 1900."[9]

While western forest reservations were created with the support of preservation-recreation groups, antagonisms aroused among some other westerners, corporations, and utilitarian-oriented interests forced the passage of the 1897 Forest Reserve Act; this act fostered *use* of the reserves, necessary in order to justify keeping the reserved lands in public ownership. President Theodore Roosevelt supported this approach and told federal foresters that while preserving the forests for their beauty and wildlife was good in itself, the prime value of the forests was in "preserving and increasing the prosperity of the nation."[10]

All the same, Roosevelt was a friend of John Muir and was a wilderness lover and publicizer in his own right. His writings, observes Nash, exhibit a love for the pioneer life, the virtue of exercise, and the beauty of the wilderness. One is led to conclude that Roosevelt, a strong supporter of national efficiency, government science, and the rational use of natural resources, also perceived certain limits to their application. In his own mind, he also reserved certain lands for wilderness, wildlife, and recreation. In a December 1901 message to Congress, he called for some of the forest reserves to afford perpetual refuge for flora and fauna, and for free camping grounds for the people. Roosevelt warmly advocated keeping Yellowstone and Yosemite National Parks "unspoiled." He lauded wilderness hunting and supported the perpetuation of wildlife by helping to create the United States Biological Survey.[11]

Foresters Fernow and Pinchot and their followers, however, had no such ambivalent approach. Hays notes that Pinchot, head of the U.S. Forest Service after 1905, sought and used the support of preservation and recreation groups, but made no effort to meet their demands. Unlike Roosevelt, Pinchot made no laudatory or effusive statements endorsing free campgrounds "for the ever-increasing numbers of men and women who have learned to find rest, health, and recreation in the splendid forests and flower-clad meadows of our mountains." On the contrary, beginning with his 1891 paper on foreign forestry, Pinchot disparaged "sentimentalism and philanthropic forest protection"; backed the logging of the Adirondack State Park in 1895; antagonized the preservationists in 1897 by asserting that sheep-grazing in the mountain meadows was harmless; and, as early as 1904, advocated the transfer of the Interior Department's national parks to his proposed forest service so that timber might be cut in them. Hays notes that bills prepared by Pinchot to accomplish this purpose were killed in the House Public Lands Committee both in 1906 and 1907. Fernow, as dean of forestry at Cornell, argued that parks and wildlife reserves were "luxury" forests and had no place in a "rational" forest policy.[12]

Pinchot continued his approach to wilderness and recreation groups, despite a 1902 revolt against Fernow's logging practices in the Adirondack Preserve (resulting in the loss of Fernow's job and the closure of the Cornell School of Forestry). When a bill to create Glacier National Park was introduced in Congress in 1907, Pinchot's Forest Service countered with its own bill, which would allow logging and other economic-oriented activities within the park. In 1908 a bill to reserve the Calaveras Big Trees in California stimulated a similar counterbill from Pinchot, which would again allow logging. Later that year Pinchot declined to invite John Muir and other preservation group leaders to the National Governors' Conference on Conservation at the White House.[13] The conference championed utilitarianism.

Pinchot was aware of the need for strong public support; he wrote in 1903 that "nothing permanent can be accomplished in this country unless it is backed by strong public sentiment." His actions, however, indicate little effort to appease or to gain the support, or at least the neutrality, of the preservation-recreation groups. Rather, he continued to antagonize all who differed with him. His attitude can be illuminated by Theodore Roosevelt's admonition given in 1901: "To go on behalf of the people much further than the people want is considerably worse than useless." Pinchot responded, "There is at least an equal danger of going slower than public opinion."[14]

7

The Parting of Ways

Two days before the 1908 Governors' Conference began, Pinchot's close friend, Secretary of the Interior James Garfield, approved the city of San Francisco's application for a permit to build a reservoir in Yosemite National Park. Pinchot had advocated approval of the permit. This action gave the preservationists a common cause to rally other national groups. Yosemite was familiar enough to influential people and associations that the ensuing conflict had the effect of uniting them into a single force and increasing their morale. The preservationists were able to fend off Pinchot and other utilitarian advocates of the reservoir for some years; they also began, in 1910, to press for a separate national park bureau. Pinchot opposed this, saying that a park bureau was no more needed than "two tails on a cat." His brother Amos labeled the park bureau supporters as peddlers of "sentimental nonsense."[15]

Pinchot's tendency to go beyond actions specifically authorized by the law led to conflict with Interior Secretary Richard Ballinger and to dismissal by President Taft in 1910. (See James Penick's Progressive Politics and Conservation for one version of the Pinchot-Ballinger controversy; other views are in books by Hays, Richardson, Pinkett, McGeary, and Pinchot.) His successor was Henry S. Graves, dean of the Yale Forestry School, who sought to mollify the preservationist-recreationist groups. One of Graves's first actions was to send a personal representative, Treadwell Cleveland, Jr., to the 1910 meeting of the American Academy of Political and Social Science. Cleveland spoke at length to the academy about the national forests' great value for recreation.[16]

In 1911 Graves wrote to the president of the Sierra Club that he was sorry if anyone had gotten the impression that the Forest Service was opposed to national park policies, and he granted his approval for a separate national park bureau. Gilligan observes, however, that this action was coincidental with President Taft's expressed desire that control of the national forest reserves, which Pinchot had succeeded in having transferred in 1905 from the Interior Department's General Land Office to the Bureau of Forestry in the Department of Agriculture, be returned to the Department of the Interior. Furthermore, both President Taft and Secretary of the Interior Ballinger had recently been persuaded to support a separate park bureau, also under the Interior Department.[17]

Graves wrote to his district foresters in early 1913:

> We all recognize that they [our forests] are going to constitute the recreation grounds of the Nation in the future. There is no

reason why the forests should not be so handled as to meet the requirements of the protection of scenic beauty. A good many of those interested in National Parks have maintained that the Forest Service is not capable of handling areas of special scenic beauty, but that they should be taken away from our jurisdiction and made into National Parks. I maintain that while certain areas like the Grand Canyon, and perhaps some of the areas surrounding certain mountain peaks may very well be placed in National Parks, the Forests as a whole can be handled so as not only to properly utilize their resources, but to make them answer also the requirements of scenic development.[18]

Graves asked the district foresters to designate areas that they thought might be future national parks, and also to identify scenic areas in the forests that should be maintained and developed aesthetically as part of the working plan for the particular national forest.

Thus, the Forest Service response to the park "problem" can be detailed as, first, an attempt by Pinchot to absorb the parks into the Forest Service and, second, acquiescence to a bill for a separate bureau—preferably under the jurisdiction of the Department of Agriculture—which also would authorize the Forest Service to provide recreation services. Although the Forest Service did, belatedly, respond to the forces of change, it failed to anticipate their magnitude. By delaying modification of its program to satisfy at least some of the preservationist-recreationist demands, it lost additional support.

The Forest Service actually did not respond until its leader had been dismissed and the welfare of the entire national forest system was severely threatened. By then it was too late to dissuade the national park movement; its supporters were polarized and their demands were cohesive.

Losing in Order to Win

The intensity of the separate park bureau struggle, with its publicity and public opinion molding, was further inflamed by the concurrent political battle going on between the preservationists and the city of San Francisco. In June of 1913, the House Committee on Public Lands held its final hearing on a San Francisco-sponsored bill to permit construction of the Hetch Hetchy Reservoir in Yosemite National Park. Gifford Pinchot was the prime witness. He strongly supported the "use" of such mountain valleys and this particular dam.[19] Forestry's chief national figure (and thus forestry) was still identified by the public as being antipark and antiwilderness.

The park preservation groups lost this battle, but the ensuing tumult and controversy created enormous publicity and national support for parks and wilderness. This attention assisted them and the newly appointed Assistant Secretary of the Interior Stephen Mather in getting the National Park Act of 1916 passed.[20] The arrival of the automobile also helped, as Mather capitalized on the surge of interest in travel to the national parks.

The independently wealthy Mather, a dynamic promoter and a wilderness enthusiast, opened up, developed, and publicized the existing parks so as to generate use and an increased appreciation of national park areas.[21] He used this base of appreciation, along with wider publicity, to add more areas to the national park system. Because many of the country's most scenic areas had already been set aside in the original forest reserve withdrawals, Mather and the Park Service soon became a political menace to the domain of the Forest Service.

Indeed, Glacier and Rocky Mountain National Parks had already been removed from the ranks of national forests, and the Forest Service soon saw more parks being proposed. By early 1917, after the Grand Canyon had passed from Forest Service control, the Park Service was recognized as a definite threat; one Forest Service official even advocated a counterattack by "popularizing the National Forests" through publicity and advertising.[22]

The Forest Service Counterattack

As the Park Service gained influence and momentum, the Forest Service also responded to the new public interest in recreation by hiring a landscape architect, issuing announcements on recreational and scenic values of the national forests, and making some isolated administrative designations of areas to be kept roadless (Trapper's Lake, Colorado, for example). This effort was particularly noticeable after the succession of W.B. Greeley to the position of chief of the Forest Service in 1920. Like Graves, Greeley believed in publicly promoting outdoor recreation as a major resource of the national forests, although policy statements sent to field officers of the Service continued to stress that recreation must be "subordinated to protection of utilization" of the forests. That field foresters tended to carry out the latter part of this policy more thoroughly than the former is revealed in the letter of resignation of the Forest Service's landscape architect (recreation engineer) in 1923. Arthur Carhart, writing to Associate Chief Forester E.A. Sherman, stated that "the [Forest S]ervice is making a mistake trying to approach everything from a board feet angle. . . . There will never be sound recreation plans in the National Forests until they are approached strictly from the side of what service they may be to human service rather than how they are going to interfere with cows and conifers."[23]

Though Carhart's comments indicate that the Forest Service was doing little for recreation at the field level, at the national publicity level Chief Forester Greeley was quite effective in offsetting the efforts of the Park Service to be the sole federal recreation agency and to acquire Forest Service lands on that account. In fact, in October 1923 Greeley secretly tried to have the Park Service transferred to the Department of Agriculture. Although this attempt was unsuccessful, in 1924 he was able to have one of his assistants, Leon F. Kneipp, appointed executive secretary of the National Conference on Outdoor Recreation, a predecessor to the Outdoor Recreation Resources Review Commission of the late 1950s. Other Forest Service personnel also served on the conference staff. Through this effort, Greeley was able to have the conference adopt a resolution which firmly endorsed recreation as a resource of the national forests.[24]

An adjunct of this three-year interdepartmental study team was the temporary appointment of a Coordinating Committee on National Parks and Forests; Greeley and Mather were both members. The chief forester lauded this coordinating committee and its method of "expert impartial analysis of each situation on the ground from the national viewpoint, not from the viewpoint of the particular local interests of whatever State it may be." Describing its establishment as an effort to develop "the most efficient correlation of Federal policies in land administration," Greeley sought to convince the National Conference on Outdoor Recreation to promote, as a permanent feature of government, the continuance of such a commission, "whose duty it is, through expert examination of particular areas, to arrive at the best solution of the administration of federal land."[25]

The existence of this coordinating committee, along with its trips to the various areas of controversy between the Park Service and the Forest Service, resulted in the diversion of some of the Park Service's political efforts out of the halls of Congress and into the committee room. The committee's existence may even have helped to blunt the campaigns of citizen groups, although the Izaak Walton League successfully pressed the Forest Service to adopt a preservation-oriented recreation plan for the Superior-Quetico area of the Superior National Forest, Minnesota, in 1926. (Later the league persuaded Congress to legislate permanent preservation of that area.)[26]

The Primitive Area Response

Although toned down, sentiment for recreation and preservation continued. Greeley still sought some way to swing preservationist support away from national parks and to the Forest Service, even though he received little support for his approach from within his own agency. For example, one high-level Forest Service official in 1925 argued that "recreation interests are a definite menace to the practice of forestry."[27]

Greeley, however, went ahead with his efforts to move the Forest Service more into the provision of recreation; and in late 1926 he established a series of administrative "wilderness areas" throughout the national forests.[28] These "wilderness"—later "primitive"—areas designated a series of existing roadless lands. He developed a set of policy statements for these areas and sent them to the field for application. These policy statements became the basis for the formal Departmental (L-20) Primitive Area Regulations of 1929.

Gilligan's research suggests that these wilderness designations and the later Primitive Area Regulations were primarily political maneuvers with a public relations purpose. Indeed, the instructions for implementing the policy and regulations were quite liberal, stating that "the establishment of a primitive area ordinarily will not operate to withdraw timber, forage, or water resources from industrial use, since the utilization of such resources, if properly regulated, will not be incompatible." Conservation publications of that time apparently believed otherwise, for they immediately began discussing the primitive areas as regions reserved for no commercial use at all.[29]

The Forest Service cannot be accused of deceit, having explained not only that "primitive" did not mean wilderness, but also that such designations could be withdrawn later. The public, meanwhile, apparently inferred that the Forest Service had changed its principles. Preservationists seemed to perceive permanence from the policy change.[30] The Forest Service then effectively countered numerous national park proposals by designating the lands in question as primitive areas under the L-20 regulations and arguing that a park was unnecessary.

12

The Battle Continues

The resignations of Greeley in 1928 and Mather in 1929 ended one rivalry. Mather had lost some possible park support by failing to officially reserve some "wilderness" in the parks; Greeley had capitalized on this by his efforts which led to the Primitive Area Regulations. He effectively cast the Park Service in a recreation developer role and diverted considerable wilderness enthusiasm to the Forest Service primitive area idea, even though there was little actual support within the Forest Service itself for such areas.[31]

Following Greeley's earlier example, the new chief forester, R.Y. Stuart, who had served as state forester for Pennsylvania Governor Gifford Pinchot during the governor's first term, wrote to the new Park Service director, Horace M. Albright, in October 1930, seeking permanent respite from new park proposals. Referring to a number of pending proposals for changes of boundaries between national park and national forest lands, Stuart complained that, in these cases, there was a "lack of orderly and systematic procedure, of clear definition of purpose, policy, standards, and of fully coordinated interdepartmental action," which seemed to militate against "certainty and soundness of decision." He suggested development of a procedure comprising congressional action, interdepartmental agreements, and, finally, review by an established citizens' advisory body "to assure that each such park proposal receives comprehensive and systematic consideration and leads to departmental and legislative decisions which will be sound and permanent." The advisory body would include a "proper proportion of persons familiar with the economic and industrial aspects of the proposals under consideration."[32]

Albright's reply on October 14 expressed interest; the director later met with Stuart, reportedly telling him that he would submit something on park standards and objectives, and also a statement on specific boundary changes. It was not until the following June that Albright submitted his proposals, and these were essentially eleven expansion projects for several different parks, at the expense of surrounding national forest lands. Stuart responded to this three different times: first, he acknowledged receipt; second, after visiting several of the areas, he concluded that statutory standards, procedures, and a rational analysis of economic considerations were still needed; and, finally, almost a year later, he explained in a seventeen-page letter all of the Forest Service's utilitarian, commercial, and economic arguments against each of Albright's proposals.[33]

However, the Park Service still had the ear of Congress. That agency's Appropriation Act for 1932, Public Law 666, contained a provision allowing the president to transfer by proclamation certain of Albright's proposed expansion areas from national forest jurisdiction to Yosemite National Park. President Hoover did just that on August 13, 1932, in spite of Stuart's expressed opposition.[34]

The election of conservation-minded President Franklin D. Roosevelt in 1932 and his appointment of strong propark Secretary of the Interior Harold L. Ickes added fuel to the interagency conflict and increased the land competition.[35]

Similar to the late teens, the 1930s became another period of National Park Service growth, with the Park Service gaining control over fifteen national monuments and both Olympic and Kings Canyon national parks from Forest Service lands. In more recent years (1950-78), Grand Teton National Park was expanded, and North Cascades National Park, Redwoods National Park, and the Mineral King addition to Sequoia National Park were all established at the expense of Forest Service domain. These land transfers have all been associated with continuing political efforts by preservation interest groups. However, the Forest Service has been politically successful in thwarting these groups' proposed Sawtooth National Park in Idaho, a controversy since 1913, and their 1975-76 attempt to add the Indian Peaks to Rocky Mountain National Park in Colorado. Recent large additions of urban seashore areas and Alaska public domain lands to the park system seem to have reduced interest in transferring national forest lands to parks.

It is the intent of this study to suggest hypotheses explaining this historic interagency conflict and to develop a theoretical model of organizational behavior. Using that model, the case of the interbureau struggle over Olympic National Park in Washington State will be examined for evidence in support or contravention of the hypotheses.

14

2

A Theoretical Model: Closed Versus Open System Organizations

The Accommodation Hypothesis

One suggested hypothesis for the obvious devotion of the U.S. Forest Service to timber utilization described in the previous chapter, which resulted in a continuing political power struggle between the utilitarian conservationists and aesthetic recreationists, is that the regulators had learned to identify with the regulated. The Forest Service was merely responding to the only constituency it had retained. Actually, this has been a continuing theme in the history of United States regulatory agencies. As Professor Grant McConnell describes it: "Once the attention of a fickle public had turned away, the lonely judicial grandeur of agencies isolated from the influences of 'politics' was vulnerable to the claims and charges of those very interests they had been established to regulate." It follows, he suggests, that over time agencies are drawn into accommodative relationships with these narrow interests. McConnell observes that "with practice, accommodation becomes a pattern." Thus, he describes the Forest Service approach to "multiple use" of natural resources as an attempt to exercise unlimited discretion in the management of public lands to suit the "personal tastes and power needs of the administrators." McConnell attributes this accommodative behavior to a lack of agency policy standards and moral direction, which leaves them open to influence, causing agency leaders to "wander before the pressures of all the winds that blow."[1]

Pointing to the importance of political power in the accommodative behavior of public agencies, as well as to their dependence on and need to build political constituencies and support, McConnell concludes that the timber production orientation of the Forest Service is perpetuated out of political necessity. The agency is simply responding to community power on the local level, "a fundamental reality of American politics."[2] The rational pursuit of power, however, should then lead to the accommodation of all strong political power, even if it comes from preservationist and recreational groups.

Research by political scientist Ashley Schiff suggests an alternative hypothesis: that subjective or ideological factors within an agency also affect that organization's power relations with its environment. Ideally, one would expect a rational organization to continually seek ways to gain public support and, consequently, to maximize its power or "solvency," as sociologist Talcott Parsons explains it. Schiff observes, however, that "power is partly a function of perception. The environment [of an organization] is filtered through layers of organizational ideology and traditions. Reality becomes relevant to organizational operations only when it is recognized."[3] Thus, an institutionalized system of belief may work against an organization to close off opportunities for responsiveness to new power sources.

The Value Orientation Alternative

The history depicted in Chapter 1 suggests that the U.S. Forest Service, rather than accommodating new power sources in its public environment, may make policy decisions on the basis of a long-standing belief pattern or value orientation, regardless of the political consequences. In any political power struggle, such a belief pattern would be expected to shape the agency's perceptions of the natural world, as well as its perceptions of its own administrative behavior. This results in an attempt to control change rather than to innovatively accommodate it.

If a value orientation can be shown to have constrained the Forest Service from responsive professional exchange with its political environment (that is, with all interested constituencies), there may be reason to question whether such an agency is capable of adapting itself to changes in public values or to new democratic pressures.

Schiff's suggestion is that value orientations, particularly toward change, scientific management, and classical economics, are responsible for partially closing off federal conservation agencies from adaptive decision making.[4] His work indicates that a normative commitment to certain values has caused these agencies to resist innovation in their administrative decisions. Because little attention has been given to studying the effects of value orientations on the administrative behavior of government agencies, this alternative hypothesis was chosen for examination.

The theoretical character of organizational values, how the organization's members acquire a normative commitment to them, and what organizational factors ensure value perpetuation are described in the Appendix. This study will examine the origin of some of the U.S. Forest Service's organizational values and the influence of those values in a transactional sequence of decision-making behavior.[5] A case study of that agency's response to new demands for wildlife and recreational land dedication in Washington's Olympic National Forest provides a chronicle of the decision process.

The Acquisition of Values in Forestry

When an aspiring forester undergoes professional training in order to qualify for membership in the forestry profession, he goes through a process of perceptually separating himself from various other reference groups (groups one aspires to be accepted by) in society. He is actually affiliating himself and identifying with one particular reference group to the exclusion of others.[6] He attends a forestry school, works summers for a forest agency, and, after successful completion of the professional training, acquires a new badge of social membership. Identifying with the members of this profession, he adopts that group's frame of reference, or value orientation, and says, "I am like them." By declaring himself *like* the other members, the individual implicitly indicates his intention to embrace that group's norms.

Organizational identification is the extent to which an individual accepts the values and goals of a system as his own, thereby becoming emotionally committed to that organization. Identification is a key variable leading to organizational effectiveness;[7] it differs from mere compliance when the individual actually believes in the opinions and actions he adopts, and does not state or perform them merely to receive favorable reactions.

Those who wish to or actually do achieve an affiliative identification with a new reference group are vulnerable to control by that group because of a fear of ostracism. Bruner has noted that "the control of identification and the manipulation of the threat of ostracism are the two greatest instruments by which human behavior is controlled by those who exert power."[8] These controls are particularly effective when the person perceives his ease of movement from the group as low.

There is little need to control a group member by threats to his identity, however, when the member has internalized the expected behavioral pattern. An individual internalizes the group's influence when the induced behavior is congruent with his own personal values. This member finds the influence rewarding and useful, and adopts it.

Internalization is further enhanced among professionals by the expectation of commitment to norms. Commitment tends to be valued when employees are considered for promotion and other rewards.

"Distinctive occupational norms thus acquire substantial moral content."[9] Values eventually become independent of the outside source and automatically guide the organization member when he is confronted with a relevant issue.

Professional men are therefore often greatly controlled by their peers through the common values acquired in the professional schools, by the constant association with other professionals in work and social situations, and by continuing education through books and journals read only by other professionals.[10]

Integrative Forces in the Forest Service

During membership in a long-standing public bureaucracy, an individual's identification with that group and his internalization of their values is further reinforced by a growing loyalty to the organization. Loyalty is engendered as a moral value to help keep the members within the organization; it is also fostered to prevent questioning of policy or organization activity, so that any criticism of accepted procedures or goals is viewed as criticism of the organization itself.[11]

When a member of an organization achieves maximum identification and internalization of the organization's values, his choices are both voluntary and have the understood approval of the organization. Later, when conflict arises and the organization represents the individual's primary frame of reference, a strong bond of loyalty has been established. This fidelity is maintained through two basic, tangible rewards: satisfaction of the human needs for approval-acceptance and for protection-security.[12]

The main basis for bureaucratic succession has become loyalty;[13] thus, all other factors being equal, this is the major determinant for promotion. Such a reward system generally yields a strong commitment to the organization's values, particularly among members who are ambitious and perceive few alternatives outside of this family.

In the federal career agencies, particularly those recruiting from only one profession, promotion is primarily from within. Either the dominant coalition within the organization or a board of ranking members appointed by it customarily makes the selections for promotions. Consequently, performance and behavior of members are heavily conditioned by those individuals' expectations of the criteria that the boards will apply in reviewing their candidacies.[14] Those promoted, therefore, tend to have adopted the value orientation of the leadership.

Candidates for promotion are sometimes more successful if they are graduates of one of the colleges or of the particular school that traditionally has furnished personnel for the agency. In several agencies, these candidates have been promoted much more rapidly and more often than persons with nontraditional training. Such reinforcement of traditional career patterns is most common when the organization is under some stress or pressure. This practice seems quite consistent with Coser's observation that groups engaged in a continued struggle with the outside environment tend to assume a sect-like character: they select membership in terms of special characteristics and demand a total personality involvement from their members.[15]

In any case, identification with a particular group and the internalization of its values are greatly strengthened by the engendering of loyalty and through the structure of the career promotion system. Nonconformists are generally weeded out before their probation ends;[16] those who remain are controlled by the pressure of supervision by older members of the agency, by attitude contagion among fellow members, by performance ratings, and by the promotion system. These integrative forces are all sustained by organization members who have completed the process or who are proceeding through it successfully.

Identification and internalization have been identified as actively utilized techniques of integration in the U.S. Forest Service.[17] In a monumental study, Professor Herbert Kaufman showed that loyalty to that organization is strongly nurtured by the kind of promotion system described above. He recognized an additional technique for building identification in the use of symbols, such as the badge and uniform. Regular and frequent transfers, particularly in the forester's early years of employment, ensure that the forester has only one reference group—the organization—in spite of far-flung field assignments and involvements in local communities. Kaufman concluded that the Service is successful in maintaining central control through its saturated, indeed almost redundant, reinforcement of identification and internalization.

Because of this, he warns: "An organization consisting of men who have internalized organizational perspectives, values and premises may well become infertile on the one hand and unreceptive on the other."[18] Innovation and change may be precluded.

Historic Influences on Forest Service Values

Kaufman did not report on other reinforcement factors bearing on the internalization of values and existential premises within the Forest Service; these include: (1) the length of time the "promotion-from-within" policy has been operating; (2) the number of years over which all decision-making positions of consequence have been staffed by forestry school graduates; and (3) the German and Prussian origins of the forestry schools and their faculties. He also failed to identify either the particular values or the existential premises underlying the basic forest regulation and administrative action models employed by the agency.

Promotion only from within, on the recommendation of one's supervisors, has been an enculturation technique employed by the Forest Service since the agency's inception in 1905. Chief Forester Gifford Pinchot observed this policy (developed under Frederick the Great) in practice in the Prussian Forest Service and described it in detail in an 1891 journal article. He concluded his discussion of the Prussian promotion system by observing that "the stimulus which ambition fails to give is supplied by the admirable esprit de corps which pervades the whole body of forest officers, and forms here, as elsewhere, the best security for the efficiency and healthy tone of the service." Other traditional German ideas for organizing a forest service were later expounded in a twenty-page letter to Pinchot by Dietrich Brandis, his former Prussian forestry professor and mentor, written in mid-February of 1897.[19]

Promotion only from within has functioned to reward behavior in the organizationally desired fashion since the time of Pinchot. Actually, enculturation for most foresters begins in forestry school. Promotion, in accordance with the values and perceptions of bureaucratic superiors, serves only to refine the process.

Before the forestry schools began to turn out sufficient numbers of foresters, another selective factor in Forest Service staffing was the examination system. Coyle describes this situation: "As for civil service examinations, no one in the government knew how to write one on forestry, or to mark the papers, except Pinchot and Graves. So it was a good team."[20]

Henry S. Graves had also studied in Germany under Professor Brandis. At one time Pinchot's assistant in the Bureau of Forestry, Graves was released by the chief forester to begin the Yale School of Forestry in 1900. Two other forestry schools had been formed: the Cornell school, headed by Bernhard Fernow, and the Biltmore school in North Carolina, supervised by Carl Schenck. The German Fernow had been trained by the great Professor Gustav Heyer in the Prussian forest academy at Muenden; Schenck, also a Prussian, was recommended for the Biltmore position by Professor Brandis. Many of the graduates of these three schools went on to staff the new Forest Service or to become the faculty of later forestry schools. Most of the Forest Ser-

20

vice's decision-making positions were filled by forestry school graduates by 1920.[21]

The charismatic leadership of Pinchot, the creation of forestry schools under his and Prussian influence, the structuring of the agency so as to maximize identification and internalization, the staffing of it with persons trained not only in the science but also in the European value orientation presented in the forestry schools—all helped to create conditions assuring the perpetuation of a particular value orientation within the agency. Favorably, the political insulation of the Forest Service in the Department of Agriculture made the agency responsible to congressional committees traditionally composed of members from nonforested farm states. In addition, its diverse clientele enabled the Forest Service to politically play one group off of another, which also helped to keep its system of values unmodified.[22]

While Kaufman observed that the professional foresters in the Forest Service had internalized the agency's values and premises for action, he did not attempt to delineate these.[23] He did state that field officers of the Service made their administrative decisions in terms of the consequences for the Forest Service. This study suggests, however, that commitment to values is so strong that agency members may make administrative decisions regardless of the consequences for the Forest Service.

Value Orientation and the Core Theories of Forestry

Whether within or without of administrative organizations, human behavior is relative to a "given" set of characteristics of the situation.[24] For an organization, these "givens" constitute a frame of reference, which involves knowledge of and assumptions about the future, awareness of alternate courses of action and of foreseen consequences inherent in these alternatives, and cognizance of a set of preferences, including values which order the consequences and the alternatives.

This frame of reference defines the situation as it appears to the rational member of the organization. It may be based on empirical fact or only partly so; however, this is not the whole story. What is important is that the frame of reference and all of its components are *believed* to be true. As W.I. Thomas knew and most sociologists since have known, "If men define situations as real, they are real in their consequences."[25]

The nonempirical part of the "reality" constituting the frame of reference for Forest Service members is hypothesized to be their particular value orientation. This includes an image of nature and of society, of the Forest Service's place in and of its relation to other parts of society, and of the conception of what is desirable and nondesirable as they relate to this system. This study will suggest that the values and the existential premises implanted in Forest Service members during and shortly after the agency's creation have been perpetuated by the structural characteristics of the organization itself. Imported from Europe, these values and premises comprise the two basic core theories of American forestry: the sustained yield forest regulation model and a special set of assumptions related to the utilitarian theories of British philosophers Sir William Hamilton and John Stuart Mill and American sociologist Lester Ward.[26]

The Sustained Yield Theory

The sustained yield theory—that is, the harvesting of no more wood than grows annually—is a European concept which has so dominated the field of forestry that Gould states it has almost stifled the development of other ideas. This theory had its start in feudal Germany, where the first efforts to control the uniformity of yield from the forest were made at Erfurt in 1359. The economic doctrine of mercantilism, prevalent in Prussia and Germany from about 1670 until the mid-1800s, adopted sustained yield because it was believed to help increase national power by providing plentiful raw material at home while reducing the need to import wood.[27]

The theory's values and premises are based on four important assumptions implicit in that early forest regulation model: (1) stability, (2) land scarcity, (3) certainty, and (4) a closed economy. According to Gould, the premise of stability assumes that an even flow of forest products is required ad infinitum. This idea has been expanded over the years into the value position that use ought to equal the rate of forest growth. Land scarcity accepts that forest products are and will continue to be so scarce, relative to labor and capital, that maximum efficient use *must* be made of all land; idle forest land is a cost to society. Future certainty assumes an unchanging technology: that production techniques, consumption patterns, and future values are all known, and a sustained yield can be planned in advance (up to 100 years or more) for a full timber rotation.

The fourth component, a closed economy, is actually a value rather than a premise, for it implies that self-sufficiency within a closed economy is desirable and that outside supplies of forest products and alternative uses of land, labor, and capital ought to be ignored.[28] This view seems related to the mercantilist position that self-sufficiency was vital to national power.

The sustained yield theory thus borrows from a two- to three-century-old European model, in which the premises of stability, land scarcity, and certainty of demand were assumed and a closed economy was valued.

The Utilitarian Theory

The utilitarian theory was conceived in eighteenth- and early nineteenth-century Europe. Within this concept, things assume utility only in terms of how they may be used by man to pursue an interest, rather than as good in their own right.[29] The value of a thing or an object depends more on what purposive use it can be put to than on its possible intrinsic value or reality. Applied to forestry, utilitarian theory has the following components: (1) timber primacy, (2) telic forestry, (3) scientific elitism, and (4) technocracy.

The timber primacy component, adapted from that described by forest economist John D. Bennett, assumes here that the first and foremost purpose of forest growth is to supply man with wood material; there is no substitute for wood and, if the forest is managed for timber, other goods and services of the forest will follow in sufficient amounts.[30]

Telic, or socially planned, forestry derives from the thinking of Pinchot's mentors, WJ McGee [sic] and Lester Ward, in the U.S. Geological Survey. As opposed to free enterprise, this concept maintains that it is the social duty of the government to control the powers of nature "to protect the water supply and regulate that balance of industries connected with woods and waters." This socialistic use of the forest was thought a desirable deterrent of the private lumber industries' destructive "boom and bust" migration policies of the mid- to late 1800s and an assurance of a stable income and a more certain future for what Pinchot visualized as "a nation of homes." Stability of the wood industry and its output ought to be the primary goal irrespective of changes in tastes, technology, consumption, and other economic factors.[31] This value, of course, meshes well with premises implicit in the sustained yield model; for example, the stability of a sustained yield-supplied community would certainly be assured if wood use were always to equal growth ad infinitum, given no change in technology.

Scientific elitism holds that a professional bureaucracy trained in science is best equipped to make policy decisions regarding natural resources.[32] It is they, rather than private entrepreneurs or the laymen of Congress, who ought to make resource allocation decisions because such decisions are basically technical in nature. The legislators, who are not technically trained, are too subject to pressures from interest groups that have no concern for scientific truth.

The component of the utilitarian theory labeled technocracy asserts that the application of professional expertise and scientific technology to natural resources, particularly forests, is best accomplished under the single and everlasting central authority of the state. Further, the application of this expertise is best achieved by specialists who exercise authority delegated to them according to impersonal rules and who are loyal only to the faithful execution of their duties.[33]

Background of Utilitarianism in the Forest Service

Timber primacy, telic forestry, scientific elitism, and technocracy also have historical roots with the Prussian mentors of Fernow, Pinchot, Schenck, Graves, and Overton Price. (Price was Pinchot's associate who also trained under Dietrich Brandis; he organized and ran the Forest Service during the many periods when Pinchot was absent. See M. Nelson McGeary, *Gifford Pinchot: Forester-Politician* [Princeton: Princeton Univ. Press, 1960], p. 47.) These values are similarly consistent with the thinking of WJ McGee. Described by Pinchot as "the scientific brains of the conservation movement," McGee greatly influenced both the chief forester and President Theodore Roosevelt. As their friend, counselor, planner, and strategist, he wrote many of Pinchot's and Roosevelt's conservation speeches. McGee was trained by Major John Wesley Powell, director of the U.S. Geological Survey and the first strong proponent of federal government resource planning and administration through science. It was McGee who transmitted the utilitarian values and premises of Powell and Ward into the twentieth-century conservation movement. Leaning heavily on the prolific sociological writings of Ward, McGee argued that it is the duty of government, through the Department of Agriculture's applied scientists, to "redirect and control the course of natural development, and the ultimate purpose is to progressively artificialize the earth with its life and growth for the benefit of men and nations." McGee further observed that the Forest Service was created "to counteract reckless deforestation and maintain the timber supply . . . while its highest duty has come to be that of . . . directing specific effort toward control over the powers of nature in such a manner as to protect the water supply and regulate that balance of industries connected with woods and waters required for the common prosperity."[34]

24

Thus, it is significant that Theodore Roosevelt spoke of the primary land policy of the United States as being "the making of prosperous homes," and Pinchot stated that the goal of conservation was "a sane, strong people, living through the centuries in a land subdued and controlled for the service of the people, its rightful masters."[35]

In carrying out the subjugation and regulation of the land for the public welfare, Pinchot held that "it is the duty of the Forest Service to see to it that the timber, water-powers, mines, and every other resource of the forests is [sic] used for the benefit of the people who live in the neighborhood and who may have a share in the welfare of each locality." He also argued that "it is only when the ripe wood is harvested properly and in time that the forest attains its highest usefulness."[36]

Pinchot seldom directly espoused scientific elitism or decision making only by experts, but this partisanship was implicit in his actions, as it was with Powell before him. He regularly attacked lay authority, and criticized politicians, stating that the nation had lost its confidence in Congress. His mentor, McGee, was more specific, advocating the idea of "directive science," with governmental experts bringing under control and redirecting all natural phenomena. McGee believed that the role of the federal department (Agriculture) was to render nature subservient to the power and prosperity of men and nations, a purpose not to be swayed "by passing opinion or popular pressure." Forester Bernhard Fernow thought that the government should not only own the forest, but it should also cut the trees and market them. Both Fernow and Pinchot argued and Pinchot wrote that "a definite, far-seeing plan is necessary for the rational management of any forest . . . ; that forest property is safest under the supervision of some imperishable guardian; or, in other words, of the State."[37]

The way to organize for dominance by the state was carefully outlined in Brandis's 1897 letter to Pinchot. He advised Pinchot to utilize both military officers and German national foresters temporarily, to be followed by a permanent force of scientifically trained American foresters, who, after college, would train for two more years in Germany.[38]

Value Orientation and Decision Making

An organization's value orientation constitutes a shared frame of reference, which includes sanctioned patterns prescribing the approved way of doing things and the established goals of that body. This orientation controls an organization's perceived purpose in society and filters its perception of public demands, excluding some as illegitimate.

In this context, organizational decision making consists of a sequence of activities carried out by agency members, whose behavior is determined by three influences: structural, informational, and shared motivational factors of the organization. In the case of the Forest Service, the shared motivational factors include both the agency's internal value orientation and a second, hidden value implicit in all organizations which serve as a primary reference group for their members: the organization itself. Thus, in the event of any conflict, all of the above values and premises comprising the Service's frame of reference would be expected to be ordered in such a way as to sustain and enhance the welfare of the organization.[39]

The second behavioral influence, informational factors, involves the external objective properties of a given situation, which will be perceived through the value filter of the organization and the existential premises which the organization *believes* to be true.

The structural factors constitute organizational roles and their relations with both the internal and the external environments. When an organization is structured to maintain a maximum of internal control— as Kaufman has shown the Forest Service in effect to be—the Merton "machine" model, or partially closed system of bureaucratic structure, should be in operation.[40]

Merton's model specifies a demand for control made on the organization by the top hierarchy.[41] This demand takes the form of increased emphasis on the reliability of behavior within the organization. Standards, procedures, and other written rules are handed down to the lower levels of the hierarchy through operating manuals and, more recently, computerized planning models. Control is accomplished through policing methods to ensure compliance with the rules.

According to Merton, this emphasis on techniques to secure reliable behavior has three consequences: (1) an increase in impersonality; (2) internalization of rules and values to the point where means become substituted for ends and instrumental technologies displace original goals; and (3) an accelerated use of categorization as a decision-making technique (such as the exhaustively detailed Forest Service operating manual) or, as Kaufman has called it, a "system of preforming decisions."[42] The decreasing search for alternatives or innovative methods of decision making corresponds to an increasing rigidity of behavior and a greater difficulty with clients.

By reasoning from Kaufman's findings, one can argue that use of this closed-system organizational model in the Forest Service seemingly has reinforced the value orientation of the Service, preventing its existential premises and values from being effectively questioned by clients, and encouraging the use of categorized, preconceived decisions. This may explain why, despite massive public involvement efforts, feedback from clients and supportive groups is treated perfunctorily or has little apparent effect on organizational decisions. For example, a study of Forest Service decision making on the Six Rivers National Forest concluded that "both clients and the staff of . . . [the] Forest have been uncertain as to what kind of input the Forest Service was seeking from clients and how the Forest Service would use this input."[43]

These structural characteristics of the Forest Service appear to preclude adaptive negotiations or decisions made through citizen participation which might anticipate or avoid potential conflicts with the agency's social environment. This behavior is typical of closed-system organizations with a bias toward certainty.[44]

A less effective alternative to anticipation of change is consolidative behavior. This type of decision making is characterized by attempts to dominate external forces for change (1) by negating or modifying them through public relations and capital expenditures and, if that fails, (2) by reordering existing, well-established programs or by devising a new program that fits within the framework of existing organizational values and norms to the maximum possible extent.[45]

This consolidative reaction to change results in an organization's being on the defensive if the forces of change overcome its attempts to control its environment. As Thompson points out, an organization that is able to anticipate institutional trends is in a much better position to exercise control of its own destiny than an organization that waits until its domain is threatened.[46]

Summary and Hypothesis

Thus, the eighteenth-century mercantilistic and utilitarian premises of stability, land scarcity, certainty, a closed economy, timber primacy, telic forestry, scientific elitism, and technocracy are argued to constitute much of the traditional frame of reference, or value orientation, of the Forest Service. If this frame of reference guided decision making in the past and precluded the influence of new public demands for allocating public forest lands for wildlife and recreational uses, then the case should follow this pattern: In the period of 1920 to 1940, the Forest Service would respond to demands for recreational land and wildlife preservation, first, with efforts to control its environment by

27

reemphasizing the Service's traditional program in light of its values and premises; second, when faced with evident defeat, it would behave consolidatively and respond to the demands by revising an existing program or by developing a new program which fit into the framework of existing organizational values and norms.

Examination of any specific political dispute of this type should disclose a reiteration of the Service's value orientation and of that orientation's continual influence on the responses made by the agency. Forest Service decision making in the controversy that resulted in the creation of the Olympic National Park from Forest Service lands will be reviewed to test this hypothesis.

Part 2   The Case Study

3

Defending the Domain: February 1897 Through August 1933

The case study presented in this and the following two chapters depicts the political defense of the U.S. Forest Service, from the perspective of its members, against the proposed Olympic national park in the Pacific Northwest. It is drawn primarily from the official correspondence files of that agency; however, other historical evidence is used occasionally to describe the situation of the foresters.

Four main streams of thought can be detected throughout the development of the case. The first is the concern over the fate of the Olympic elk. This concern, which had been a primary factor in the 1909 establishment of Mount Olympus National Monument under President Theodore Roosevelt, resurfaces again and again throughout this history.

Second, there is renewed focus on closure of the area to mining, a restriction that had been in effect since the establishment of the monument. While initially instrumental in generating support for change, this element seems to fade away gradually.

Third, the interest in and enthusiasm over the recreation and tourism potential of the area—plans for mountain climbing and stream fishing, and appreciation of the natural beauty and the wilderness— also central in the decision to establish the monument, continue to build in importance and prominence, particularly in the last part of the study.

Fourth, there is a continuing agenda for utilization of the resources, especially the timber. Forest Service values in this area are regularly reinforced by various business and local groups.

This chapter covers the early history of the Olympic controversy. The reader will notice several references to the hypothesized values and premises of the Forest Service, particularly in the arguments over the 1916 national park bills. These references reappear in discussions on the development of national forest timber management plans in the early 1920s and in the various exhortations of District Forester Christopher M. Granger later in that decade. During this early period, there was a continual reappearance of the national park idea, stimulated by both the elk problem and recreation interest; this, however, did not get very far. The Forest Service policy of utilization appears to have been dominant, although it was not accepted unquestioningly.

The Resource

The political struggle for the Olympic Forest involved agency jurisdiction over and uses to be made of federally owned lands lying in the northwest corner of the state of Washington. This area, known as the Olympic Peninsula, is located between the Pacific Ocean and Puget Sound, and contains some 6,500 square miles of public and private lands. The peninsula is roughly square and is about 80 miles across. About 3,000 square miles of the land area are covered by the Olympic Mountains, a cluster of steep peaks and small ranges divided by deep canyons or narrow valleys and covered with snow and glaciers at the higher elevations. The mountains rise to over 7,900 feet; their western slopes have the wettest climate in the continental United States (up to 200 inches of annual precipitation). Interestingly, lands lying just to the east and northeast are relatively dry, with from 16 to 25 inches of annual rainfall. Most areas from sea level to 5,500 feet elevation were originally covered with some of the heaviest coniferous forests in the country.

The central part of the Olympic Mountains is only sixty-five miles from Seattle, with its metropolitan area of more than a million persons. Along the outer, coastal edges of the peninsula itself are various smaller communities, with populations ranging from a few hundred to about 30,000 residents. Commerce and industry in these towns have generally been dependent upon the lumber and the pulp and paper industries, with the fishing trade playing a smaller role; however, the largest community, Bremerton, is dominated by United States naval facilities. Tourism in these once-isolated lands has become quite important in recent years, especially since the completion of the highway bridge, stretching across the mouth of the Columbia River to the south, making access to the peninsula easier and less circuitous for highway travelers.

Major lumbering from the sea (there were no railroads yet) began on the peninsula in 1853, when the first experienced New England timbermen discovered the region. Most of the land on the peninsula was originally in the public domain, and the early mills acquired their logs in an open market from various settlers. Presumably, the settlers had homesteaded the land or entered it under other federal land laws; but by 1875 lumber firms had acquired large holdings of their own in order to be assured of future timber supplies. It is reputed that a large portion of these lands were acquired fraudulently under the Timber and Stone Act, in dealings analogous to the Oregon land frauds described by S.A.D. Puter.[1]

Though visible from Seattle, the public lands on the Olympic Peninsula were protected by the lack of roads and railroads. Thus, they remained open to land entry claims and private acquisition until President Grover Cleveland proclaimed the Olympic Forest Reserve on February 22, 1897. This reserve of 2,188,800 acres was created under the authority of the 1891 Forest Reserve Act. Many protests were voiced about the size of the reserve, however; and on April 7, 1900, President William McKinley reduced the reserve by 264,960 acres. A second proclamation by President McKinley, on July 15, 1901, further reduced the reserve, returning another 456,960 acres to the public domain. Gifford Pinchot, then chief of the purely information-gathering Bureau of Forestry in the Department of Agriculture, complained that "nearly every acre of it passed promptly and fraudulently into the hands of lumbermen." Four years later, however, Pinchot and the new president, Theodore Roosevelt, succeeded in obtaining legislation transferring this and the other reserves from the Department of the Interior to Pinchot's bureau in the Department of Agriculture. Roosevelt restored 127,680 acres to the Olympic Forest Reserve on March 2, 1907, as part of his famed midnight withdrawals.[2]

The Cushman Bill, 1904

The first official effort to change the public forest reserve lands in the Olympic Mountains into a national park was made in 1904, when a bill was introduced in Congress to establish an "Elk National Park" on the Olympic Peninsula.[3] Introduced by Representative Francis W. Cushman of Tacoma, Washington, the bill was in response to wildlife enthusiasts' concerns about alleged wholesale slaughter of the native Olympic elk, the *Cervus roosevelti*. The elk were being killed by poachers who sought their teeth for the Fraternal Order's watchfob ornaments. Cushman's bill, however, did not pass.

Another interest group appeared in August 1907, when sixty members of The Seattle Mountaineers visited the still-isolated and little-explored Olympic Mountains. This party from the newly formed climbing and outdoor group spent some two weeks exploring the area, conquering peaks, and taking pictures. Some of the members had spent much of the previous two months building trails so that the larger party would have easier access. The group returned to Seattle pondering some way to preserve the area. In early 1909 the club requested that the Washington State congressional delegation consider the Olympics for national park status.[4]

The National Monument, 1909

Meanwhile, the U.S. Biological Survey had recommended a national monument withdrawal to protect the breeding grounds of the Olympic elk from roads and from mining and logging; this recommendation was opposed by the Forest Service chief law officer.[5]

On March 2, 1909, Representative W.E. Humphrey of Tacoma drafted a proclamation for Theodore Roosevelt's signature which would withdraw the Mount Olympus National Monument.[6] The presidential proclamation was issued the next day, and soon thereafter settlers and miners began to object to the 600,000-acre national monument.

Forest Service District Forester George Cecil was in charge of all forest reserves (later renamed national forests) in Oregon and Washington. That July he requested that the monument be abolished. However, Acting Chief Forester* C.S. Chapman rebuffed him in deference to the Biological Survey, which "would very decidedly disapprove."[7]

The district forester pressed the issue again in the following year, hoping that the Biological Survey would accept establishment of a state game refuge in lieu of the monument. Cecil wanted to correct the appearance that the Forest Service might be "fostering hunting grounds to the exclusion of the development of the natural resources" of the area.[8]

Henry S. Graves succeeded Gifford Pinchot as chief forester on February 1, 1910. He, too, denied the district's request because of

*The title "chief forester" is used throughout this study to refer to the chief executive of the Forest Service. Before the mid-1930s the title was "the forester"; in that decade it was changed to "chief." His assistants, formerly called "associate foresters" and "assistant foresters," became the "associate chiefs" and "assistant chiefs," respectively. District foresters were the equivalent of the present regional foresters, having supervisory authority over fifteen to twenty individual national forests, each headed, as they are now, by a forest supervisor. Other titles remain as they were at the time the reference is made.

opposition by Dr. T.S. Palmer, chief of the Biological Survey. Graves informed Cecil that "I shall be very glad if you will bear in mind the promise made Dr. Palmer." Miners, anxious for the release of the monument, were to be advised to take the matter up directly with the Biological Survey.[9]

In 1911 Olympic Forest Supervisor R.E. Benedict again suggested abolishing the monument, arguing that, while its intent was to preserve the breeding grounds of the elk, these grounds were largely outside of the monument. District Forester Cecil supported this argument in a seven-page letter to Chief Forester Graves; he urged abolishment of the Mount Olympus National Monument "because it doesn't support the elk and is preventing the use of resources."[10]

The First Humphrey Bill, 1911

Other forces were also at work. Another national park bill for the Olympics, using the monument boundaries, was introduced by Representative Humphrey on July 15, 1911. District Forester Cecil quickly asked for a staff report on the timber and other values in the area. In a twelve-page letter to the chief forester, he again argued that the monument was ineffective for elk protection and he suggested that the loss of the area's notable mining and timber values was an excessive price to pay for protection of the land for elk or for scenic beauty.[11]

A new forest supervisor, P.S. Lovejoy, had meanwhile begun to oppose the Humphrey bill for a laundry list of reasons. He felt that the bill would hamstring the administration of the forest; would tie up resources; wouldn't protect the elk; would only serve to open the present monument to mining; would mean an inefficient duplication of administration; and would withdraw fifty million dollars of timber (market value) from certain future "proper and necessary development." He believed that one timber sale had already been made within the monument and others were planned. The district forester commended Supervisor Lovejoy's assessment to Chief Forester Graves and said that a great quantity of resources would be rendered "useless."[12]

Later in the year, Lovejoy reiterated his opposition to a national park because of the many billions of board feet of "splendid timber" which should be open to development. He also suggested alternatives to the existing Mount Olympus National Monument for protecting the elk winter range.[13]

The Seattle Mountaineers, however, continued to press for a park; and Representative Humphrey encouraged miners, farmers, and

Mountaineers to get together and agree on a boundary. A meeting was held on December 19, 1911, and boundaries were agreed upon for a park about half the size of the existing monument.[14]

The chief forester, apparently acquiescent to Humphrey's park bill, advised the district of some boundary adjustments suggested by the Biological Survey. These changes provided exit corridors for the elk to their winter range. He asked the field personnel for any suggested modifications to the Biological Survey proposals. Lovejoy objected to the proposals, maintaining that the "Monument in no manner has or could protect the elk," and adding that the heaviest stands of timber include the best winter range of the elk within the national forest. He said:

> The Survey's proposed Wynoochee extension of the National Park . . . would permanently close the entire drainage to util-ization of the timber stand. . . . The recommendations of the Seattle Committee of miners, Chamber of Commerce people, and The Mountaineers were carefully considered and endorsed by practically all of the commercial organizations and interested persons throughout the Northwest.[15]

Commercial groups throughout the state later endorsed a pamphlet published by the mining interests, which proposed a park to be taken from part of the monument and mining of the land. A modified version of the Humphrey bill was introduced as Senate Bill 5257 by Senator W.L. Jones of Washington in the 62d Congress, 2d session. Because the park boundaries set forth in the bill were consistent with the present monument, however, the bill was opposed by the Forest Service district forester, who wanted the timber excluded also.[16] It eventually failed to pass.

In 1914 the miners, by way of the Washington congressional delegation, put pressure on Secretary of Agriculture D.F. Houston for the elimination of the national monument. Houston's response to the delegation was that no recommendation countermanding the order of a former chief executive could be made to the new president, Woodrow Wilson, without a thorough investigation. Chief Forester Graves then asked for a report on what the district was doing to protect and administer the monument.[17]

The new supervisor of the Olympic National Forest, R.L. Fromme, responded that the monument was of practically no concern to the administration of the national forest except that it was exempt from mining and that agriculture was discouraged.[18] Fromme also noted that he was often hard put, sometimes "vanquished," to find a satisfactory reason for the creation and existence of this large, special withdrawal

36

within his national forest. He added (as previously reported by his predecessor, Lovejoy) that one timber sale within the monument had been conducted in 1911 and that others were planned. The elk were adequately taken care of, he said, by state game laws, which closed the elk season until 1925.

Chief Forester Graves planned a fall trip to the Olympics to examine the area and to hear all interested groups. He so advised Congressman Albert Johnson of Washington.

The Monument Reduction, 1915

Upon his return to Washington, D.C., Graves composed a twelve-page memorandum that discussed the monument's effectiveness in terms of its stated functions; he also predicted a future need for its timber. He recommended that the monument be reduced by one-half, reserving the more scenic portions (which he described as being certain unique features of interest to visitors and pleasure-seekers) for further consideration as a national park.[19] A bill to establish a national park bureau was being considered by Congress at that time.

Graves later told District Forester Cecil about the Forest Service solicitor's opinion that the Service had the legal authority to deny agricultural entry on those national forest lands outside the monument which had value as elk breeding grounds. This was to become a prime argument in persuading the Biological Survey to support the size reduction of the monument. Graves also advised the district forester of his intent to recommend to the Department of the Interior that the remaining monument land be made into a national park.[20] (This was probably done in order to get the necessary Interior support for the proposed reduction.) Stephen Mather, the Interior Department's new assistant secretary for parks, was reluctant to agree to the size reduction but wanted to establish a basis for cooperating with the Forest Service.[21] These actions led to President Wilson's proclamation, on May 11, 1915, which reduced the area of the Mount Olympus National Monument by one-half.

Graves visited Seattle again that summer, en route to Alaska, and conferred on July 20 with Forest Supervisor Fromme and attorney George Wright of The Seattle Mountaineers. Graves hoped to guide Mountaineer agitation for recreation accessibility in the Olympics into appropriation support for Forest Service trail building, rather than for the early creation of a park. He told Wright and commercial photographer Asahel Curtis of Seattle that the question of a park depended on the joint consideration of both agencies and that the Forest Service would wish to exclude the heavy bodies of timber from the park. He said that the Forest Service would go ahead and plan a system of trails and roads within the monument. Graves also suggested that Wright and Curtis get in touch with Mather and Mark Daniels of the Interior Department, and invite them to visit the Olympics. Mather came to see the Olympics in August 1915, after touring Mount Rainier National Park.[22]

Years later Horace Albright, director of the National Park Service after Mather, testified before the House Public Lands Committee (May 1936) that both he and Mather had judged the Olympics of park caliber in 1915, but that they did not want to press the issue too hard because they were trying to "establish a basis for doing business with the Forest Service."[23]

At a conference of various Washington commercial clubs held in Seattle on November 18, 1915, a resolution to Congress was passed that favored a change in the status of the present monument to that of a national park. This resolution had originated in the Federation of Women's clubs and had been amended, by Mountaineer attorney Wright and two representatives from Port Townsend, to include the near 7,000-foot peaks of Mount Constance and The Brothers, both located to the east of the existing monument. However, opposition to any change in the existing monument boundaries came from photographer Curtis and was supported by two of his fellow Seattle Chamber of Commerce representatives.[24] (Curtis, a "booster" of commercial development and road building, figures strongly as a Forest Service supporter later in this case.)[25]

After the developments at this meeting, Olympic Supervisor Fromme concluded that it was not so important to push the chief forester's trail plans. Instead, Fromme went ahead and planned several road-building projects at an estimated cost of about $465,000, including one which would bisect the monument along the Elwha and Quinault rivers. He considered these roads to be of urgent importance, "particularly in the interests of recreation and . . . administrative efficiency."[26]

Upon receipt of Fromme's plans, however, Graves informed the supervisor that a bill now in Congress for the creation of a bureau of national parks would place all national monuments under the the the wing of the Interior Department.[27] Noting that the Mount Olympus National Monument "may pass out of our jurisdiction," the chief forester advised against spending Forest Service permanent improvement funds within the monument and used Fromme's recommendations instead as a basis for a special appropriations request.[28]

The 1916 Park Bill

Another factor that added caution to Graves's outlook was the introduction of a new park bill on January 4, 1916. This bill allowed mining within the proposed Olympic park, as did the previous one.[29]

In spite of political pressures from miners, wildlife lovers, and recreationists, the local foresters had moved ahead with a timber management working plan for the Olympics. Dated March 18, 1916, the plan inventoried the timber stand at about 89 billion board feet and noted that the 1915 annual cut on the forest had increased to more than 12.5 million board feet. The plan stated that "the chief function of the National Forests is the furnishing of a continuous supply of timber" and then continued:

> To efficiently handle the disposal of timber within the Olympic National Forest, careful analysis must be made of the various bodies of timber, the communities most affected by its method of removal so as to insure permanency to present established localities, the markets which will of necessity consume the production, and the grade of material which will be produced. . . . It is highly desirious [sic] to place the Forest on a sustained annual yield basis of management rather than on a periodic yield, because of its large extent in area, the immense body of timber ready for immediate cutting, and the desirability of securing a steady industrial development in the region.[30]

The utilitarian foresters' beliefs in timber primacy and in the obligation of the Forest Service to ensure the development and permanence of dependent forest industries was further bolstered when Olympic Supervisor Fromme sent a detailed memorandum to the district forester telling why the monument should not be transferred to the Interior Department. He asserted that the present management method under a single agency was more efficient; thus, costs of administration, travel, road and trail construction, and resource utilization were cheaper. He went on to state that "development of the interior Olympic Mountains for fire protection, [for] economic utilization of resources, and for recreation demand total disregard for the Monument boundaries if the public and local industries are really to be best served."[31]

Commenting on the House version of the Olympic national park bill, Fromme argued: "There is no doubt of a decided local sentiment in favor of a National Park in the Olympic Mountains, but its administration can be most economically and efficiently conducted by the Forest Service in connection with the surrounding National Forest, rather than introducing the active interest of a separate Department."[32] The district forester passed Fromme's argument to Washington, stating that "from the topographic standpoint, economic standpoint, and recreational standpoint, the Monument and the surrounding forest land are a unit . . . and less economic waste will occur under one management." He admitted that the Olympic Mountains do offer attractions "warranting intensive development along park lines, and the opposition of this office is directed to the change in jurisdiction rather than the creation of a park."[33] Furthermore, Fromme argued that a national park "confined to proper territory cannot protect the winter feeding and calving range of a reasonable sized herd of elk." And, if the park were larger, "it would seriously conflict with the utilization of merchantable timber."[34]

The Olympic bill died in the House Committee on Agriculture, after Chairman A.F. Lever received a letter opposing it from Secretary of Agriculture David Houston. Houston argued that the Forest Service had included recreational development of the monument in its plans; that a park would be more expensive; and that it was impossible to consider this particular problem without confronting the whole policy of creating parks out of national forests. He noted that even with his recommendation of the Grand Canyon for a national park, differences in viewpoint had developed (between the Agriculture and Interior departments) "leading to the need for broad general principles for handling Parks and Forests first."[35]

The Elk Problem Looms

The death of the 1916 Olympic park bill and the advent of the First World War, with its demands for spruce lumber from the Olympic Peninsula for airplane construction, quieted the recreation enthusiasts for a time; but die-offs (mortality due to winter starvation) of the Olympic elk continued to cause the Forest Service problems. A special report to the Washington office of the Forest Service in late 1917 emphasized that many of the elk problems were beyond the Service's control: the winter range of the elk was outside the monument; severe winters were causing heavy calf losses; and it was uncertain whether the number of elk would increase. A study by the Biological Survey was requested.

Late in the following spring, Vernon Bailey of the Biological Survey investigated and found that the recent elk deaths "could have largely been prevented by gently scattering the elk or urging them down the

[Hoh River] valley past the three ranches." Estimating elk numbers at seven to eight thousand, he said there was room for almost twice that number on the national forest lands, and recommended hunting by special permits only. The Forest Service and the Biological Survey conferred in January 1919 and agreed on legislative implementation, through the state, of Bailey's recommendations;[36] however, the Elks Lodge of the state succeeded in blocking the proposed legislation.

Meanwhile, heeding the counsel of landscape architect Franklin Waugh, the Forest Service had been demonstrating nationally that it was involved in the recreation business.[37] The Olympic National Forest followed suit by developing plans for summer home sites on Forest Service land around Lake Crescent, aesthetically locating the access highway and making efforts to exchange lands near the lake to minimize visible logging scars. Water power development with draw-down effects on the lake was opposed by the Forest Service.[38] Finally, a recreation plan for the Lake Crescent area was completed by recreation engineer Fred Cleator and was submitted to Waugh for advice and comment.[39]

These commendable efforts were apparently too little and too late. In November 1922, the board of trustees of the Seattle Chamber of Commerce sent a resolution to both Forest Supervisor Fromme and the new chief forester, William B. Greeley, requesting that the Forest Service step up its land exchange efforts because the beauty of Lake Crescent was being destroyed by the logging of private timber around its shoreline. Fromme assured the chamber of commerce that further land exchanges would be investigated as the property became available, but that landowners were not likely to make a reasonable exchange for timber elsewhere. Though Assistant District Forester C.J. Buck suggested that Fromme be more aggressive in his response than merely answering letters, little in the record shows that this suggestion was followed.[40]

Fromme was still occupied with the elk die-off problem. He had been appearing before sportsmen's groups and Elks Lodges, and even before the state trustees of the Elks Lodges, advocating a bill in the state legislature to provide for elk hunting to help control overpopulation and winter starvation. Fromme informed the district forester of his efforts, noting that he intended to push such legislation only to the point of representing the views of the Biological Survey and the Forest Service, both of whom favored a system of eliminating a few male elk in limited congested localities. He observed that due to public concern about the elk, the support of some senators was doubtful; and the Game Commission, the Elks Lodges, and some county groups were opposed to any elk season. Indeed, the Sportsmen's Association of

Clallam County, which contained part of the Olympic National Forest, had only two days before decided that they opposed any legislation permitting the killing of elk on the Olympic Peninsula until a census had been conducted by the Biological Survey.[41]

Local fears about the elk population persisted, and were apparently related to the continued poaching. The 700 some members of the Hoquiam Rod and Gun Club passed a resolution in August of 1921, which objected to tooth hunters and urged making the possession and wearing of an elk tooth a gross misdemeanor.[42] In the following spring editor E.B. Webster of the *Port Angeles Evening News* wrote a sharply critical article about the Forest Service's handling of the elk situation. Soon thereafter Congressman Albert Johnson spoke to the U.S. House of Representatives about the slaughter of the elk in the Olympic National Forest. However, Webster later reversed his stand. After visiting the Hoh Valley with Forest Service personnel and finding starved elk, he wrote a more sympathetic article about the Forest Service's handling of the problem.[43]

Timber Versus Recreation

Thus, except for reacting in piecemeal fashion to individual pressures and problems relating to both recreation and wildlife, the managers of the Olympic National Forest failed to anticipate or extensively plan for either future recreation or wildlife management. Seemingly in accordance with the foresters' beliefs in the primacy of wood production and the future scarcity of timber, this staff made plans only for complete utilization of *all* timber on the Olympic National Forest. The timber management plan for the Olympic National Forest was issued on May 1, 1923, over Supervisor Fromme's name, and made no mention of the existence of the national monument. Yet, the timber from *every watershed* within the monument was included in the estimate of available saw timber. The 1924 Revised Timber Management Plan, by R.L. Fromme, recognized the national monument, but still included all of its timber within described working circles. For example, it stated that "compartment 10 in the above table is within the Mount Olympus National Monument. . . . The timbered area embraces no features that removing the timber would destroy. . . . Compartment 11 in the Elwha, Block XIV, is within the boundaries of the Mount Olympus National Monument. . . . Removing this timber would in no way conflict with the purposes for which the Monument was created."[44]

These timber management plans appeared to be quite consistent with the attitudes expressed by Supervisor Fromme's superiors in the Portland district office. In the April 1925 "in-house" newsletter of the district, *The Six-Twenty-Six,* District Forester Christopher M. Granger told his staff that

> the one foremost purpose of the Forest Service [is] to develop the National Forests to their highest usefulness. . . .
>
> Boiled down, the essence of what we are all working toward . . . is continuous production. . . . Continuous production on the National Forests obviously means organizing our timber assets into logical units, each of which will furnish a sustained yield capable of supporting an economic manufacturing unit. . . . In addition to the simplification and stabilization of our activities, there will be a stabilizing influence on prosperity and the upbuilding of permanent communities of forest workers.[45]

Here, in a nutshell, several of the core values and premises of forestry were expressed: timber primacy, stability, future certainty, a closed economy, and telic forestry.

Granger asserted one more organizational value—that only government could accomplish the professional application of forestry expertise—when he told his employees that "we have the job of spreading the gospel throughout all of the timbered region adjacent to the National Forest so that eventually private forestry will be on the same permanent basis. . . . We feel absolutely certain that the public is prepared to receive and digest the gospel of continuous production."[46]

In the same issue of *The Six-Twenty Six* it was noted that "there is some excitement at times over the invasion of wilderness areas by roads, especially on the part of wildlife enthusiasts. We have very far to go yet before we reach the standards of German forests." Later in that publication, Assistant District Forester J.G. Guthrie wrote:

> Forage is one of the many resources of the National Forests for which the Forest Service is responsible to see that are put to the highest and and best use—to be *used,* not preserved *from* use. . . . Stockmen pay the American people for the forage they make use of; . . . the hunter pays only the license fee for his pleasure . . . by his hunting he makes only a comparatively slight contribution to the total food supply of the Nation; and food and raiment are more important than pleasure in the life of a nation.[47]

Meanwhile, on the national level, Chief Forester Greeley had been diverting much of the national park system expansion efforts of Service

Director Stephen Mather away from Congress and toward the Coordinating Committee of the National Conference on Outdoor Recreation. However, Greeley was not entirely successful in reducing all park proposals to "rational considerations"; the May issue of *The Six-Twenty-Six* observed there was "considerable agitation for the establishment of a National Park south of Wallowa Lake" (Oregon). Elsewhere, aesthetic recreationists had been protesting the timber cutting along scenic roads, but one voice in the *The Six-Twenty-Six* chastised them: "It has been noted that our sight-seeing friends do not camp in the big primeval woods. . . . Then, too, there is the object lesson of growing a new forest to replace the one cut. I believe that alone is worth the few years it takes to clothe those naked areas with another stand of trees." However, the Forest Service seemed ambivalent when its "sight-seeing friends" put up their own funds for recreational development of the Olympic National Forest. In August 1925, *The Six-Twenty-Six* commented that "Nineteen businessmen from Hoquiam and Aberdeen hiked into the Low Divide to fish and climb nearby Mountains. . . . It is understood that this group will incorporate for $25,000 to build a chalet on the Divide."[48]

The Johnson Bill and Entry of Eastern Elites

The spectre of a national park appeared again in June of 1926 when Washington Congressman Albert Johnson introduced a new park bill and it was referred to the Committee on Public Lands.[49] Faced with this threat, the Forest Service apparently decided to reverse its previous response to citizen concerns about the elk. Assistant District Forester Buck initiated a legal inquiry into whether the Forest Service had authority, under the Antiquities (National Monument) Act, to establish a game refuge or to prohibit hunting and trapping within the monument. He was advised by the agency's assistant solicitor, M.F. Staley, that no such authority existed.[50] The refuge idea waned temporarily after the park bill died in the committee.

One year later the seeming impotence or unwillingness of the Forest Service to protect the Olympic elk prompted F.W. Mathias of the Hoquiam Rotary Club to write a long letter of complaint to Charles W. Folds, chairman of the National Executive Committee of the Izaak Walton League. Lamenting the highly political county control of the Washington state game system, Mathias declared it was a crime not to protect this "most glorious recreational area" forever. He insisted that the Forest Service had done nothing to protect the area, and had instead made efforts to prevent preservation. Someone "suggested that the Izaak Walton League could lend great assistance."[51] The league enjoyed a strong political position at that time, having only the year before pressured the Forest Service into making an administrative reservation of Minnesota's Boundary Waters Canoe Area; this group was later responsible for congressional passage of the 1930 Shipstead-Nolan Act, which required the Forest Service to preserve the Boundary Waters lakes.[52]

Folds passed Mathias's letter on to Park Service Director Stephen Mather, along with his own letter of inquiry. Mather referred both letters to the Forest Service.[53] Additional inquiries about the elk protection program came from Washington's Congressman Albert Johnson and Senator W.L. Jones, who both had also received letters from Mathias. The Forest Service replied directly and through the Secretary of Agriculture, pointing out that even though hunting did not appear to be restricted within the monument, the elk habitat was protected against land appropriation; that failure to create a game refuge had not seriously endangered the elk; and that the Forest Service would be glad to consider asking Congress for a federal game refuge in the Olympics if this was desired.[54]

This 1927 exchange of correspondence with Mathias apparently prompted the district office to raise the elk issue at the September annual meeting of the Western Association of State Fish and Game Commissioners in Seattle.[55] The matter was then allowed to rest for two months, until Congressman Johnson made a follow-up inquiry into the Department of Agriculture's offer to recommend the refuge.[56] Johnson was anxious to determine the desirability of introducing such a bill in the forthcoming session of Congress. At this point, however, District Forester Granger dismissed the idea, explaining that the state was now considering small refuges of its own. He noted that "a large number of matters relative to recreational improvements, wilderness areas, the construction of roads and trails, and other administrative subjects are somewhat involved and require serious study of the whole area with a view to the careful correlation of the various uses. . . . The question of a federal game refuge should be deferred until this general plan has taken more definite form."[57]

The Service was reacting defensively to pressure again. This time their reaction was the so-called "Cleator Plan," a broad master scheme for the monument and its surrounding peaks and waters, prepared by recreational engineer Fred Cleator of the Portland district office. This plan mapped out roads and trails throughout the Olympic Mountains, with corridor strips reserved from timber cutting along these pathways. It also outlined a future, 134,000-acre primitive area of high peaks adjacent to the monument, redesignating the monument itself as the "Snow Peaks Recreation Area." Completed in 1928, the plan was subsequently used in arguments against the Olympic park bills sponsored in Congress. Fred Cleator later told a state review committee that his plan "was done under the multiple use policy of the U.S. Forest Service, not as an argument under [sic] a National Park, but with the knowledge that the Olympic Park was under consideration."[58]

These efforts of the Forest Service, however, were insufficient to quiet or divert the complaints by Mathias and the Izaak Walton League. In October 1928, the influential Madison Grant, president of the New York Zoological Society and a founder of the Boone and Crockett Club, raised the question of an Olympic National Park with Stephen Mather. Grant noted that "the forests there are magnificent and the Forest Service is considering cutting the trees down in the immediate future." The Forest Service immediately reassured Mather and Grant that they were planning a proper development of the recreational resource and had designed no highways in the higher sections of the Olympic Mountains.[59] Such assurances were somewhat vacuous when compared with the actual written timber management plan.

Timber Takes the Spotlight

Additional demands for the timber were developing while the elk controversy smouldered. Northwest timber magnate J.H. Bloedel approached Chief Forester Greeley about commitment of the Olympic Forest timber in the Hoh and Bogachiel watersheds to his company's planned ten million dollar pulp mill, to be located across Puget Sound in Bellingham.[60] Two years later, in 1929, a special committee from various Grays Harbor communities to the south presented the Forest Service with similar demands for the allocation of timber in the Hoh, Bogachiel, and Queets watersheds of the Olympic National Forest to their timber-short mills. The upper portions of these watersheds were in the monument. The Simpson Timber Company of Shelton and the Bloedel-Donovan/Merrill-Ring timber interests in the north objected to any allocation to Grays Harbor. In an April meeting, District Forester Granger told assembled Grays Harbor interests that the Forest Service had approached the "matter from the standpoint of strong desire to play a part in building up community stability, that being one of our major considerations in our policies relating to the disposal of the forest resources; and we were much more concerned with this than getting the highest possible stumpage price."[61] Doubting the wisdom of allocation to Grays Harbor alone, Granger proposed withholding timber in the three sought-after watersheds from sale until a common-carrier railroad was built so that all interested parties could bid competitively.

The day after this meeting, J.J. Donovan and J.H. Bloedel called upon District Forester Granger to confer over the Grays Harbor request for preferential allocation. They argued that the timber from the Hoh and Bogachiel Rivers could be taken out to the north to Puget Sound mills more cheaply than to Grays Harbor. However, Granger later decided to retain his timber withholding idea for the west Olympics pending the construction of the common-carrier railroad, and offered instead to put 850 million board feet of timber from the Satsop River area in the south Olympics up for sale at a sustained yield rate. This idea was approved by the new chief forester, Major R.Y. Stuart.[62]

Preoccupation with the timber production potential of the Olympics dominated Forest Service thought throughout 1929. Even recreation land exchanges on Lake Crescent were being examined with an eye toward how much of their public timber could later be logged to help pay for the exchanges. The proposed Fairholm exchange, for example, could yield fifty percent of its standing volume to the Forest Service's annual cut, according to the new forest supervisor, Herbert L. Plumb.[63] In addition, Forest Service responses to congressional inquiries about the Mount Olympus National Monument advised that its margins included a great deal of timber with high commercial value.[64]

The Forest Service generally seemed little concerned about recreation in 1929 and early 1930. An examination of the committee reports of the Forest Service Regional Foresters' Conference (held in Washington, D.C., from March 17 to April 9, 1930) and the accompanying commentary by the chief forester reveals that of 101 lithographed pages, only 1½ pages dealt with recreation and only half a page with game management, while forty-five pages were concerned with internal administration and twenty-four with fire and timber management.[65] A recreation planner was suggested by the committees for the chief forester's office, but the regional foresters advised that no such planners, particularly landscape architects, were needed in the regions. (Note here that the districts and district foresters have now been renamed as regions and regional foresters.)

The Primitive Area of 1930

Even in responding to suggestions from the Washington office for implementing the L-20 Primitive Area Regulations of 1929 (see

47

Chapter 1), logging possibilities were a paramount consideration for the Region Six staff. The chief's office had proposed a primitive area contiguous to the existing Mount Olympus National Monument and C.J. Buck, recently promoted to regional forester, sought the advice of Portland's Rodney Glisan, civic leader and president of the Mazamas Mountaineering Club, regarding the proper location of the boundaries of the proposal. Buck was worried about the possibility of strenuous objections from "the nature lovers" when, as he put it, "the time came for invasion and necessary cutting within the boundaries of the Primitive Area." He was considering exclusion, therefore, of all fingers of valley timber that projected into the rock peaks of the primitive area. Glisan, however, recommended including the fingers, thus making the boundary more easily marked and observed.[66]

Thus, the Forest Service's "Report on the Olympic Primitive Area" of November 5, 1930, indicated that there were 13,000 acres of merchantable timber within the newly reserved, 134,000-acre primitive area. The report's "plan of management" discussed the proposed utilization of these timber resources and stated: "Utilization of merchantable timber in the low valleys that project into the Area is intended by this plan; but so far as possible without destroying or seriously interfering in the primitive aspect of adjoining lands."[67]

In early 1931 The Seattle Mountaineers inquired about the official interpretation of the term "primitive" and asked if any roads were planned in the primitive area. Forest Supervisor Plumb replied that the primitive area would be left in its natural state so far as was possible, with only one through road (over Anderson Pass from the Dosewallips River to the Quinault River). Plumb described the Mount Olympus "Snow Peaks Recreation Area" (actually the monument, but arbitrarily renamed) as a "wilderness" area; he added, however, that it was possible to log merchantable timber in both the primitive and recreation areas, "but this [logging] will be done without destroying or interfering with the primitive aspect of adjoining lands." Plumb also stated that a through road had been considered for the proposed recreation area, following the Elwha River and the north fork of the Quinault River, but this was not confirmed.[68]

These loopholes in the presumed protection afforded by the primitive area were unsettling to The Mountaineers and helped to stimulate their later strong support of a new park bill. It was not uncommon for aesthetic recreation groups to interpret the rather vague primitive area policies as completely protective, but, as James Gilligan has clearly shown, Forest Service field men interpreted the policies as allowing administrative roads and timber cutting, and fully intended to carry out such plans.[69]

48

Eastern Influence Continues

Meanwhile, a New York associate of Madison Grant, who may well have inspired Grant's original 1928 letter to Steve Mather, was having an impact on the outcome of the Olympic park controversy. Willard Van Name, an associate curator of the American Museum of Natural History, traveled throughout the West in 1928, examining both national parks and lands for potential parks. His *Vanishing Forest Reserves* was then published in 1929. This book was highly critical of the Forest Service and of the nonaggressive, and in fact accommodative, attitude of the Park Service toward the Forest Service. Van Name was particularly critical of the Park Service for not seeking more land for parks in the state of Washington.[70] (The author of the subsequent pamphlet published by New York's Emergency Conservation Committee proposing an Olympic park,[71] Van Name later testified in the 1936 House hearings and, in 1937, persistently pressed the Forest Service for Olympic timber-cutting information.)

A special Forest Service file of correspondence with the American Museum of Natural History about the Olympic elk began in mid-1930 after Van Name's book was published. The idea of an Olympic national park, both for scenery preservation and as a solution to the elk question, again stirred national interest. This time, the park idea had such impetus that Assistant Chief Forester L.F. Kneipp admonished the Forest Service Washington office staff: "National Forests have nothing to fear from National Parks if their administration is so ordered that it most fully meets public desires. The probability that large areas of National Forest land will be transferred to National Parks is most acute in those instances where the Forest Service refuses to recognize a well-defined demand on the part of the public." There was a crescendo of staff complaints about Kneipp's views, with the majority also questioning the primitive area policy.[72]

National Pressures Increase

The National Park Service was quick to seize the initiative. The group's new director, Horace M. Albright, wrote to the Forest Service in June of 1931 to describe ten sizable parcels of national forest land that he wished to add to existing national parks. Chief Forester Stuart responded with a lengthy letter to Albright in October 1931, and again in March 1932. His first letter sought to reduce the park transfer question to a computational decision-making procedure using standards and definitions drawn up by the professionals in the two agencies. He went on to propose that these criteria then be legitimized by congressional sanction or interdepartmental agreement.[73]

Stuart's second response to Albright detailed in seventeen pages the numerous utilitarian and "economic" reasons why each of Albright's proposals should be rejected. This letter revealed much of the value orientation of the Forest Service and, reiterating the need for maximum administrative efficiency, spoke repeatedly of timber stands "not now of economic significance because of inaccessibility but destined eventually to have significance as other more accessible supplies are exhausted" and of timber located where "the most complete utilization of timber consistent with sound public interest is essential to maintain the economic life of the dependent communities." Stuart argued that "if . . . economic use of water, forage, timber, and other resources is to be allowed in *proper coordination with the scenic element,* the area should remain in its present status as a part of the National Forest." Expert studies leading to a "sound determination of the principles under which this area will contribute most to the social progress and public welfare" would both point the way to formulation of a specific policy and plan for the future management of the territory.[74]

These arguments apparently did not satisfy either Albright or Congress, as the transfer of the first of the sought-after lands, the Wawona area of Yosemite National Park, was soon authorized by a rider attached to the Interior Department's Appropriations Act. Unaware of the rider, the Forest Service was surprised by a presidential proclamation of the transfer on August 13, 1932. It was noted in the minutes of the Service Committee (chief forester's staff meeting) that "the Department of Agriculture was not consulted in this transfer as required by a previous National Park Service commitment."[75]

Besides the revived aggressiveness of the National Park Service, there were other pressures influencing the Forest Service's response to the Olympic national park movement. The country's economic depression had led to a strong preoccupation with economy and efficiency in the federal government. A bill in Congress in early 1932 proposed a total reorganization of some agencies. To facilitate the activation of public works projects, the reorganization bill called for a transfer of some existing agencies, or the construction-related arms of those agencies, to a proposed public works administration. The proposal included the road, trail, and facilities construction functions of the Forest Service. A revision of this bill was finally passed as the Economy Act in June 1932, giving the president the authority to regroup agencies (these regroupings were subject to a congressional veto within sixty days). This aggregation authority was followed by another, more severe proposal the next January, when Senate hearings were held to consider aggregation of all federal conservation activities.[76]

Easterners Raise the Elk Problem Again

The Forest Service—now forced to fend off conservation groups interested in scenic and elk preservation on the local level, and reorganization enthusiasts and the Park Service on the national level—continued to develop its plans for sustained yield timber production in the Olympic National Forest. Working circles were laid out and timber land allocated with an eye to interesting "the most logical operator" (the Simpson Timber Company) in contracting for federal timber. Additional concerns about the efforts of Grays Harbor operators to "maintain their largely over expanded mill capacity" were expressed.[77]

However, concern for the elk by New York's American Museum of Natural History and other groups continued. Dr. H.E. Anthony, curator of mammalogy and chairman of the Boone and Crockett Club's Olympic Peninsula Committee, asked the Park Service whether a national monument was an inviolate wildlife sanctuary. Theodore Roosevelt's son Kermit also contacted Chief Forester Stuart about the status of the Olympic elk. Dr. Anthony wrote again. The Forest Service responded that no wholesale slaughter of the elk was being planned, but that an attempt was being made to cooperatively work out the problem of overgrazing with local interests.[78]

Of course, compounding the Forest Service's problem with the elk was its desultory and impromptu approach. The elk and other wildlife were not part of the agency's value orientation. At that time wildlife was not really considered a forest product and had been left traditionally to state jurisdiction. Even though the monument had been proclaimed to protect the elk, this was a unique application of federal policy. Whether the elk were diminishing as a result of poaching or overpopulation seemed to be a matter of opinion, and, although the Forest Service did not feel responsible, the agency was perceived to be negligent. Therefore it was not surprising when, on November 7, 1932, the Olympic Peninsula Development League passed a resolution to President Herbert Hoover that read:

> WHEREAS: the Olympic elk are a community asset,
>   We deplore the slaughter that has occurred in alarming proportions,

51

State and County funds are not available for the protection of the Olympic elk,

The Mount Olympus National Monument was created primarily for the purpose of protecting the elk,

BE IT RESOLVED that we request the President to take action that will assure the protection of the elk in the Monument and in the National Forest.[79]

The resolution to the president was referred to the secretary of agriculture, who, after a one-month delay, responded that management of the elk was considered a state responsibility. The Forest Service and the Biological Survey were happy to cooperate, the response went on, and a well-planned investigation would be made. Actually, meetings between the Biological Survey and the Forest Service had taken place in the previous two weeks, and the Survey, attributing the elk deaths to overpopulation, now advocated more hunting, not more protection.[80]

This approach pleased neither F.W. Mathias nor the Olympic Development League. While waiting for an answer from President Hoover, the league had Mathias mail a copy of the resolution to Dr. Anthony. Mathias added that many elk were being killed and left to rot, and that unless some branch of the federal government took action soon, the herds would be decimated.[81]

Mathias also sent a copy of his letter to Anthony to Olympic National Forest Supervisor Plumb, who forwarded it to the regional forester. Plumb wrote: "I am informed that Congressman Smith [from the Grays Harbor area], who defeated Albert Johnson, is planning to introduce a bill for the creation of a National Park. . . . As there will be a meeting of the Olympic Peninsula Development League on December 1, I would like your ideas on this matter." Assistant Regional Forester F.V. "Jack" Horton, seemingly unconcerned, replied: "I doubt very much whether under the present economic conditions, a national park can be created, when it is fully understood that this will call for additional outlay of federal money."[82]

Plumb then wrote to Mathias, describing the detrimental effects such a park would have on local communities and resources. He portrayed a park as a *non-use* and also as a monopolistic development of special scenery.

In this country . . . where economic and industrial needs ultimately will require coordinated use of every available resource, the correlation of recreation with forest management is even more desirable and necessary than elsewhere. Upon areas not of national park caliber . . . [that] form of administration is inconsistent with a desirable use and enjoyment by the people of publicly owned lands, with economic and industrial welfare particularly of local populations, and with administrative economy. . . . Recreational use is not inconsistent with forest management, but to the contrary is a common byproduct of such management.[83]

Supervisor Plumb's arguments, however, did little to change the course of events in the beginning of 1933. Mathias had already revitalized the interest of the eastern wildlife groups. In early January Chief Forester Stuart received an invitation to appear later that month before a Senate Special Committee on Conservation of Wildlife Resources. The hearings, chaired by Senator Frederick C. Walcott, were to consider consolidation of federal conservation agencies under a single cabinet officer. The subject was derived from the previous year's reorganization bill proposals for efficiency in government. At these hearings Stuart was forewarned of things to come by the testimony of Rosalie Edge, secretary of the Emergency Conservation Committee of New York City and the leader of that group, who eventually would come to the forefront of the Olympic park battle. Mrs. Edge opposed aggregation of the Forest Service and the Park Service through any reorganization because, as she remarked, the Forest Service's hostility to the Park Service "makes it a menace to the National Parks." She accused the Forest Service of gaining power quietly through "wasteful sale of timber and grazing rights."[84]

Also in January Chief Forester Stuart received a letter from T. Gilbert Pearson, the president of the National Association of Audubon Societies, asking for the records on recent law enforcement efforts to protect the Olympic elk from unlawful hunting. Stuart responded apologetically with statistics indicating a poor record. Stuart also wrote, belatedly, to the regional forester in Portland, requesting recommendations for improving future law enforcement efforts on federal lands in the Olympics. A few days later, Dr. Anthony wrote again to Stuart, saying: "If illegal killing of the Roosevelt Elk is going on, we deplore it and hope that something will be done about the matter." He enclosed some resolutions passed by the Boone and Crockett Club, noting that they were not intended to be a reflection upon the various government and state offices involved, but represented instead "an attempt to develop an investigation and discussion of a situation which is disturbing people who live in the region in question." Stuart responded that the Forest Service would welcome the assistance of all organizations uniting on a common plan of administration. "It is in our judgment a cooperative project."[85]

The interest of national wildlife groups persisted in January, with the Audubon Society pressing for more information and the New York Zoological Society sending resolutions to numerous governmental figures and entities, including the Forest Service and the Park Service, which called for an investigation of the threat to the existence of the Olympic elk. The society also noted that it might soon recommend extension of federal protection under a national park, monument, or wildlife sanctuary.[86]

Chief Forester Stuart wrote to the New York Zoological Society, telling them that the Forest Service planned a complete investigation and sought cooperative counsel from the society in preparing final plans.

On January 26, 1933, New Jersey Congressman Charles A. Eaton introduced a bill that provided for the transfer of the Forest Service to the Department of the Interior.[87]

The Berry Petition

In the previous fall, the *Port Angeles Evening News* had carried a story entitled "Roads Penetrating Olympics Opposed by California Man." John E. Berry, a California businessman and an outdoor enthusiast, had been visiting the area and had become interested in the Olympics, so he decided to remain in the Hoquiam area. In March 1933 he wrote to the secretary of agriculture on Hoquiam Chamber of Commerce stationary, enclosing his "petition" to the secretary to add certain scenic lands to the existing national monument and primitive area. Assistant Chief Forester L.F. Kneipp referred Berry's petition to the regional forester, after writing to tell Berry that "permanent economic justification and physical preservation of the Primitive Areas depend upon their logical correlation with the economic requirements of the Regions of which they are a part." The regional office in turn passed Berry's petition on to Supervisor H.L. Plumb, suggesting that Plumb contact Berry and warning that a comparable primitive area battle had begun two years ago with just such a start.[88]

Plumb responded to the regional forester by dismissing Berry as an agitator who did not represent the Hoquiam Chamber of Commerce. He proposed that Buck reply to Berry, stating that the recreation plan for the Olympic Forest had been made after study by competent authority, that the Forest Service's policy was to work in close cooperation with the Olympic Development League, and that it could give little consideration to individual opinions. Berry, however, had sent copies of his petition to several outdoor groups, and the Mazamas suggested that their members endorse Berry's petition. Regional Forester Buck hurriedly requested an opportunity to talk with the Mazamas before they took such action; at the same time, while ignoring Plumb's proposal, he again admonished him to make personal contact with Berry, whose influence may have reached other groups. He reminded the supervisor that "our greatest Primitive Area controversy, still going after two years' action, had a very insignificant start." Plumb replied that he had heard that Berry was attempting to get the Sierra Club to make a trip into the Olympics, but that he still saw no necessity to contact Berry personally.[89]

The regional forester met with the Mazamas on May 3. He followed this encounter with a very conciliatory letter, offering to have one of his staff members attend future regular sessions of the Mazamas and asking if he might arrange a meeting between key Mazama members and the chairman of the House Committee on Public Lands. The Seattle Mountaineers, who up to this point had not openly endorsed Berry's proposal, began now to take an interest in the eastern turmoil about the elk. They wrote to the chief of the Biological Survey, telling him that they were disturbed by reports of a possible hunting season on the Olympic Peninsula.[90] The letter was referred to the Forest Service. Assistant Chief C.E. Rachford responded to The Mountaineers, telling them that a cooperative management plan was being developed and suggesting that they contact local Forest Service officials.

The Park Service Gains the High Ground

While the Forest Service was thus preoccupied in 1933 at both the local and national levels, a presidential action was taking place that would greatly affect the Olympic National Forest. The Economy Act, which had passed in June 1932, remained in force for two years. President Hoover first used it before leaving office in December 1932, to propose a sweeping reassignment of bureaus. Congress refused him, however, the House Democratic majority preferring to allow the newly elected president, Franklin Roosevelt, complete freedom to perform his own reorganization. Although the new president did not live up to early expectations in this regard, he did issue seven executive orders under this act, which, for the most part, brought about only minor changes.[91] Neither the Park Service nor the Forest Service, however, were immediately aware of the occurrence of one significant change.

Executive Order 6166, issued on June 10, 1933, combined the administrations of numerous battlefields, cemeteries, and public buildings and placed them under the National Park Service. An additional portion of this order transferred all national monuments, including the Mount Olympus National Monument, to the Park Service (renamed temporarily by this order as the Office of National Parks, Buildings, and Reservations). The Forest Service appears to have become aware of this executive order shortly before August 16, 1933, two weeks after the sixty-day contesting period. On that date, Assistant Chief Forester Kneipp wrote to Buck as follows:

> As you doubtless know, the President's Executive Order of June 10, *re* reorganization of certain Government units technically placed all National Monuments under the National Park Service. In an effort to secure an interpretation of the Order, the matter was taken up with the Budget Bureau, which took it up with the Park Service. The National Park Service indicated a desire to take over eight of the fifteen National Monuments now administered by the Forest Service. How long it will be before they ask for the other seven is wholly conjectural. Apparently they have the high ground on us under the Order.[92]

Summary

Throughout this early history of the Mount Olympus National Monument, it is evident that the Forest Service perceived the land and its forests primarily as a source of timber supply to cope with an impending scarcity of timber. In providing for that certain future need, the Service held that timber must be used in such a fashion as to maintain continuous production forever, while at the same time developing and stabilizing local forest industries and communities. The elk population and scenic preservation were considered less important issues; hence, the forces of change generated by these issues were not anticipated and planned for in advance. These lesser concerns gathered overt and organized forces to which the Forest Service was, in the long run, compelled to respond defensively. This was a typical consolidative response pattern.

However, as Gawthrop notes, an organization's choice between anticipating external pressure (and hence retaining the ability and opportunity to creatively control and guide its effects) and operating within a frame of reference that emphasizes institutional certainty, behavioral stability, and conflict avoidance may not actually be a free choice.[93]

Rather, the decision is imposed on the organization as a result of the nature of that body's value structure.

That such a consolidative response pattern, as well as the traditional value preferences of the Forest Service, seems to have been perpetuated within the agency is suggested by this early history of the Mount Olympus National Monument. We would now expect to find, as the Olympic conflict continued to escalate, that organizational values and perceptions were still articulated clearly and firmly, and that decisions were made without equivocation. This should be so, even though "the action chosen entails great costs in the sense that it will deny realization of previous goals and challenge important beliefs."[94] With another agency competing with the Forest Service for land jurisdiction on the same "turf," we would expect these traditional, institutionalized values, styles of response, and perceptions of the situation to be used to resist any inroads.[95] An increased threat to the foresters' domain could be expected to heighten the rigidity of their response.[96] Such a threat was now present at the grass roots level, as competition for the Forest Service's traditional local support suddenly emerged upon the scene because of the monument's transfer to the jurisdiction of the Park Service.

4

The Struggle for the Olympic Forest: August 1933 Through April 1936

In this chapter you will read about a three-year episode of interbureau rivalry not unlike others. The National Park Service's claim to a legitimate area of jurisdiction caused considerable political competition and much conflict for the Forest Service. Taking an aloof stance, the Forest Service suddenly found itself in the middle of a mounting public relations campaign, carried out by representatives of the Park Service, who sought grass roots support for increasing their jurisdiction in the Olympics. While the elk situation continued to draw public criticism to the Forest Service, mining pressures gradually disappeared. The drive for recreation and scenic beauty received new vigor from Secretary of the Interior Harold Ickes.

The Forest Service chose to fight these threats by emphasizing its telic view of forestry. In the midst of a glutted paper pulp market, the agency attempted to stabilize and perpetually sustain several local communities dependent on this financially shaky industry. It reasserted the primacy of timber production as a forest use. Only when President Roosevelt personally intervened in the dispute, obviously taking the side of the preservationists, did the Service back down. Then, assuming a consolidative approach, the agency belatedly responded by increasing the size of the Olympic Primitive Area, reluctantly withdrawing a substantial amount of old-growth timber from commercial use. Still, even in the document proclaiming enlargement of the primitive area, one finds a strong emphasis on the "shortage" of timber and the importance of the lumber industry, rather than on recreation and preservation.

The Monument Transfer

The first reaction from Chief Forester R.Y. Stuart's office to the possible transfer of the Mount Olympus National Monument to the National Park Service was to ask the field staff to sound out local reaction to a "Roosevelt" national game refuge proposal. When Supervisor Plumb sought local opinion and reported on it, however, he was rebuked by Regional Forester Buck, who stated, "Keep this material confidential. If we do anything we will simply build up a lot of trouble for ourselves this winter, centering particularly around Olympic National Park agitation."[1]

Buck warned the chief forester in Washington that any proposal to alter the status of the monument would be likely to precipitate further park proposals, with "endless meetings, newspaper editorials, and correspondence." He said that many local people believed they had a preserve of considerable value to the community. Noting that the elk matter had created a tempest among state and local centers, Buck concluded that even "settled policies, which appear well supported by the public, such as the establishment of a Primitive Area, are subject to intermittent questioning."[2] This referred to the 1930 designation of a 134,800-acre Olympic Forest Primitive Area along the east side of the monument.

On September 28, 1933, more than six weeks after the final date to contest the executive order that transferred the fifteen national monuments to the Park Service, the subject finally came up in the chief forester's staff meeting. The topic was labeled "Possible Transfer of National Monuments," and the discussion mentioned that the Park Service was interpreting the order to mean that jurisdiction over the fifteen monuments would pass to them on October 1, 1933. The regions were not notified of this transfer, however, until Regional Forester Buck made an inquiry in mid-October. Chief Forester Stuart telegraphed Buck to report: "Interior Department has construed Executive Order June 10, 1933, as giving it jurisdiction over all National Monuments. . . . Since jurisdiction is being actively asserted by the Interior Department, you should in interests of harmony advise state officials and public to comply with requirements that department until decided otherwise."[3]

Meanwhile, the Forest Service, in following the suggestions of experts in the Biological Survey, had been promoting an open elk season on the Olympic Peninsula to protect the winter range from overgrazing. Stuart responded to an inquiry from Dr. Anthony in early October, writing that the contemplated open season scheduled for October 19 through 22 was consistent with the two federal agencies' suggested cooperative investigations. The Boone and Crockett Club then hired naturalist M.P. Skinner to observe and report on the hunt, in which 157 bull elk were killed. Skinner's two reports criticized both "political" State Game Commission and Forest Service game surveys, estimating at least twenty percent damage to the elk herds because of many elk illegally wounded and left to die. He blamed domestic animals for the overgrazing on the Hoh River Valley and accused the Forest Service of grossly underestimating the number of cattle and sheep on the national forest. Skinner then recommended a three-year study by the best available biologists; he also advised that the monument area be enlarged and made into a national park to protect the elk range.[4]

The sudden death on October 23, 1933, of Chief Forester Stuart—an apparent suicide—preempted Olympic concerns in the Washington office and left the Forest Service headless for nearly a month. An assistant regional forester sent a handwritten note to Assistant Chief Forester Kneipp on November 1 that read: "Just to add to the general confusion and uncertainty, we find that very apparently the Park Service has designs on the Olympic." Forest Service personnel had encountered Dave Madsen of the Park Service watching the elk hunt. Madsen had commented that the monument should "doubtless" be extended to include Quinault and Crescent lakes, with the former making a fine headquarters.[5]

The Washington office's response indicated that the Forest Service had not been consulted about the executive order that transferred the national monuments to the Park Service, and that they were thinking about making an open complaint to Congress or to the president. It was felt, however, that an interdepartmental issue might be undesirable at this time, primarily because the secretary of the interior, as administrator of the Public Works Programs, had control of many funds and projects under the Department of Agriculture. "Open dissension between the two Departments," the message said, "conceivably would complicate developments along those lines." There was also concern over how the president might react to any move to counter his order. Thus, the Washington office counseled patience, diplomacy, and avoidance of friction, "as under the terms of the [executive] Order the Interior Department has a strong color of authority for its present action."[6]

Nevertheless, in the period before his death Chief Forester Stuart had undertaken a series of efforts to retrieve the monument for the Forest Service, including bringing the matter up personally with President Roosevelt. The president had shown an appreciation of the situation and had suggested that the matter be worked out with the secretary of the interior.[7] However, arranging a meeting with Secretary Ickes had proved difficult, and the death of Stuart undoubtedly complicated matters for the Forest Service.[8]

Prospects of losing jurisdiction over the Olympic Monument elicited unhappy comments from the Region Six staff. Assistant Regional Forester Fred Ames lamented to the Lands Division that the transfer was a very serious problem from the standpoint of the Division of Forest Management because more than three billion board feet of timber were tied up by the action and could not be harvested. "The creation of the National Monument to provide a game refuge for the elk had no bearing on Forest Management activities, since timber within the Monument was available for cutting and management plans were not affected. . . . It is urged that every possible effort be made to except [sic] this Monument from the Executive Order."[9]

The March 1934 *Timber Management Plan Policy Statement* for the Olympic National Forest confirmed Ames's implication that considerable monument timber was scheduled for logging.[10]

Still, politics would prevail over telic forestry. Secretary Ickes, consolidating his position, stated his interest both in transferring the Forest Service to the Interior Department and in extending the National Park system.[11] He concluded that the Forest Service would not give up "an inch of land anywhere it could avoid it."[12] The national monument jurisdictional question remained in abeyance until Ickes settled the matter in a public announcement at the end of March 1934.

The Push for a Park

It was now obvious that Park Service officials were also interested in turning much of the Olympic National Forest into a park.[13] In May of 1934, one further complication entered the Forest Service's problem with its domain.

That month the Emergency Conservation Committee of New York City began distributing a pamphlet called "The Proposed Olympic National Park." This committee was chaired by Rosalie Edge, who had participated in the January congressional hearing. Regional Forester Buck sent a copy of the pamphlet to the new chief forester, Ferdinand A. Silcox, and pointed out that:

> Just who appointed or inspired this Emergency Conservation Committee is not clear from the pamphlet, . . . [which] insinuates malfeasance on the part of the Forest Service. . . . The plea on the back for the transfer of the monuments to the Park Service . . . may give some indication of who is backing this agitation. In view of such distributions, it seemed desirable for the Forest Service to take a hand. I am enclosing material used in a talk by me in Aberdeen, May 22.[14]

Responding for the chief, Assistant Chief Forester Kneipp described the Emergency Conservation Committee as primarily inspired by the "almost fanatical" Van Name of the American Museum of Natural History. Kneipp added that the Emergency Conservation Committee made its appeal "to the ultra-sentimental and emotional elements," which had "some following but not a large one." He also expressed his conviction that the Park Service was "quite receptive to the idea of having the entire Olympic Peninsula in a National Park," a situation he deemed of sufficient gravity to warrant definite and constructive action. Approving Buck's arguments to the Grays Harbor Chamber of Commerce in Aberdeen, he encouraged continued presentations until "there is complete understanding of the whole situation" by the local people now neutral or in favor of a park. He advised Buck to "use the deadly parallel to make your case. The right man in your office could visit various towns and Chambers of Commerce, sit down with them, and with a little arithmetic show them alternative costs and returns."[15]

Buck had cited a number of the Forest Service's values in his Aberdeen speech. Decrying what had happened in past decades to the private timber resource on the Olympic Peninsula, he argued that industry should "plan ahead, like a forester." Further, he proposed that "every acre of the thousands outlying should be producing five hundred B. M. log scale Scribner [volume of wood] per acre per year." The speech called for "permanence of communities in a planned economy," and Buck concluded:

> The proposed Olympic National Park is merely a matter which must be handled along the line of greatest human welfare in land use planning. From a community standpoint it [the timber proposed for a park] would mean year-long employment for 600 men in the woods and 600 more family men working in five mills with 120 thousand per day cut, 200 days a year. A total community of 1200 families from now until Gabriel blows his horn.[16]

Following Kneipp's advice, the Forest Service stepped to the defense of its domain. Names of board members and the financial status of the Emergency Conservation Committee were obtained from George L. Drake of the Simpson Logging Company, with the aid of the New York office of the American Pulp and Paper Association.[17] Information was gathered from both Park and Forest Service sources about present National Park Service policies toward summer homes and private inholdings, and also about total resort income, investment by private operators, and numbers of employees supported both by the resource and sport fishing in other parks.[18] Subsequently, the Forest

Service used this material to raise questions in the minds of local citizens about the potential economic impact of national parks on tourism income. Because of considerable propark sentiment in Port Angeles, Supervisor Plumb also appeared before the local Chamber of Commerce to discuss both the Emergency Conservation Committee pamphlet and the economic facts.[19]

Meanwhile, Irving Clark, the Seattle attorney for The Mountaineers, had written to the Forest Service urging an enlargement of the monument. In his response of May 29, 1934, Buck reiterated some of the Service's values mentioned in his Grays Harbor address. He reminded Clark of the 1,200 "family men" to be supported forever by the timber in the present monument, adding that all the timber from the Olympic Peninsula would be required in the future (ad infinitum) to supply logs for various mills in the area. Asserting the primacy of timber, he then reassured Clark that careful planning and regulation of logging would preserve recreational values without injury to either the lumber industry or the scenic features.[20]

A stepped-up Forest Service publicity campaign emphasized the conservation of natural beauty and the maintenance of primitive conditions as demonstrated by the primitive area set aside in the Olympics; it did not mention any future intent to log that area. In addition, forest supervisors and regional office staff members attended and addressed meetings of the Washington State Planning Council.[21] At one of these meetings, an assistant regional forester noticed different propark interests favoring various degrees of development. When the Park Service remained noncommittal on the matter, the Forest Service was put on the defensive. To counteract this, Plumb was advised by his superiors to encourage his "key-men" (friendly community and business leaders) to get National Park Service personnel to commit themselves publicly as to which type of development they had planned. The Forest Service believed the local people would become openly divided on this issue and reject a park.[22]

Plumb was later told to "keep all Forest Service action which might be controversial out of any public discussion of the Park question."[23] In accordance with this, the regional office decided in August of 1934 that it was not advisable to make public the findings of an elk study by Olaus J. Murie of the Biological Survey, because the study recommended further reduction of certain elk herds.[24] Plumb was instructed to present his arguments against a park from a "land use planning angle," and was given comparative national park figures to be kept confidential but to be used in "holding estimates of economic benefits from a proposed park to reasonable limits" in his discussions with key-men.[25]

Telic Forestry Versus the Park

The basic reason the Forest Service wished to retain jurisdiction over the entire peninsula was first expressed in a letter from Chief Forester Ferdinand Silcox to Ovid Butler of the American Forestry Association, in which Silcox noted: "During the period of adjustment [because of private overcutting] the timber resources of the Olympic National Forest will be a major factor in maintaining the established [industrial] structure and the social institutions it supports."[26]

The Forest Service planned to use the promise of government timber as a carry-over to induce timber-famished private companies to acquire and reforest their own private lands in the area. The Forest Service believed the amount of such reforested private lands would be limited only by the portion of government timber it could promise to provide in the interim.[27] The existence of future markets for both public and private timber was taken for granted, apparently, as no mention was made of investment required or of any future return rate, even in the later detailed sustained yield unit planning.[28]

In the summer of 1934 the Park Service was busy trying to maintain and improve its local image. One representative, Dave Madsen, was observed by Plumb as spending a large amount of time being a "good politician" with people known to be favorable to the park idea. Madsen tried to minimize the Forest Service-Park Service conflict and to place the onus of the park proposal on the Emergency Conservation Committee.[29] Forest Service regional officials felt the Park Service was playing down the conflict in order to disarm local interests, thereby more easily accomplishing the congressional action needed.[30] When the Park Service's Washington office photographer arrived and began taking pictures of national forest areas outside the monument, Plumb expressed concern to the Park Service. The supervisor got the impression that Park Service officials might use the possible unlawfulness of President Wilson's 1915 monument reduction "as trading stock" to get what they wanted.

Assistant Regional Forester Jack Horton complained to Kneipp, in a handwritten note marked "personal and destroy," that the "Olympic National Monument [sic]" movement was a *real* movement now; he went on to say that

> Madsen is sure doing his stuff. . . . He is a slick gent. I know of no way to combat the method now being used by the N.P. Service unless it be to hire a "slicker" of our own. I don't want to do that.
>
> Madsen has unlimited time to spend building up favorable

sentiment and he is a past master at disarming opposition. We, the Forest Service are at a decided disadvantage. . . .

There is no use kidding ourselves about the final issue in this case. It will not be decided on the basis of logic or sound business judgment. It will be decided on sentiment and emotion. At the present time any change looks good to the businessman. Things have been and still are so bad that any change would look as though it might be better.[31]

Horton had previously complained to Kneipp about an unannounced topographic survey of Forest Service lands around Crater Lake National Park being done at the request of the Park Service. Kneipp responded:

The National Park Service now is probably at the zenith of its power and prestige. It has a Secretary that supports it aggressively and unquestioningly and who also happens to be the Public Works Administrator with the control of huge allotments of funds. It seems willing to take chances that we in the Forest Service will hardly dare to take. An intensive topographic survey of a five mile strip around a single national park apparently is only a minor feature of the present program.[32]

Consequently, when Horton wrote again about the problem of counteracting Madsen's work in the Olympic area, Kneipp observed:

Frankly this National Park situation is assuming new aspects and rapidly developing new conditions which may compel new points of view on the part of the Forest Service. After all, the management of Federal properties must conform to the principles and policies enumerated by the Administration. . . .

Another factor influencing the situation is the change in the economic status of timber production, the now apparent certainty that large areas of inaccessible forests will not be required for industrial purposes for a long time in the future, if ever.

. . . why should the Forest Service worry about ceding supervisory control over certain relatively limited areas of outstanding natural beauty . . . not indispensable to the economic life of the Nation?[33]

Kneipp, as noted before, was somewhat alone in his views among the Forest Service staff. His was the only heretical view denying future timber scarcity found among Forest Service foresters in the entire case. Perhaps this was because of his original specialty in range management rather than timber management before becoming involved with Lands and Recreation. His words fell on deaf ears in Region Six, where field personnel continued to contend that, as an integral part of the national forest, Mount Olympus National Monument would be better economically administered by one agency, and that severe economic losses would ensue if logging were excluded. They reiterated that the Forest Service was in the recreation business, too, but the timber was needed to sustain the stability of local communities until private sustained yield units could begin to furnish commercial timber again.[34]

Madsen's public relations efforts included the generation of propark editorials,[35] about which Buck complained: "This sort of publicity makes it extremely difficult to secure consideration of the Monument problem on the basis of reason and determination of economic values." Assistant Chief Forester Kneipp wrote to Buck in December 1934: "We cannot hope to compete with the National Park Service in the concentration of high pressure salesmanship on local communities or the creation of hopes of unlimited wealth to be derived from some new form of land use, nor should we wish to do so if we could. We can, however, prepare or encourage the preparation of definite factual statements susceptible of ready verification by local interests."[36]

Therefore, Plumb and the regional office staff continued to stress the amount of saw timber in the present monument, as well as the additional thirteen billion board feet in the larger park proposed by the Emergency Conservation Committee. The dependence of the Olympic Peninsula and its cities on pulp, paper, shingles, and logging was also emphasized. Also, the importance of the local twenty-five percent share of national forest timber receipts was reiterated. Recreation was pointed out to be very seasonal, and the local people were reminded that national parks were havens for predatory animals and that "park concessioners have never made any money on their investments."[37] The Forest Service calculated that 1,000 men could be employed perpetually in logging the additional timberlands proposed for a park; the duplication of federal administration of forest lands on the peninsula was asserted to be more costly; and multiple use of the resources was said to be of best advantage to the public, as well as providing the most efficient management.[38]

About this time the Forest Service obtained copies of a new Park Service field team's park proposal, recommending the addition of 110,000 acres to the monument—less than that proposed by the Emergency Conservation Committee. The Forest Service described this new park plan as no more feasible an administrative unit than was already in the monument, likening the proposed improvements to those which would have been made by the Forest Service and arguing that the resulting duplicate administration of one area would be illogical and costly. They also believed the Park Service, once established in the area, would not be satisfied for very long with the smaller acreage, particularly with recreational use going on in the country surrounding the park.[39]

The Park Service later modified its recommendations to conform with those of the Port Angeles Chamber of Commerce. This joint proposal was sent to Washington State Congressman Monrad C. Wallgren and to senators Homer Bone and Lewis Schwellenbach in February 1935. Following the presentation of the new park plan to the Olympic Development League, Plumb explained the Forest Service's ideas about sustained yield to the group, stressing that elimination of such a large body of timber from cutting would seriously affect the sustained yield program.[40]

Horton wrote to Kneipp, advising him of the Port Angeles Chamber of Commerce's position and noting that other communities might flop to the side of the Park Service upon the return of that agency's people in the summer. Horton continued: "I do not share your optimism that right will prevail and am convinced that the decision on this case, if not all cases, will be based largely on sentiment and feeling, rather than 'hard cold facts.'" Kneipp responded:

> I am not unaware of the fact that emotion and sentiment will dominate reason and logic. Nevertheless, in this issue, reason and logic must be our sole defensive. We cannot very well afford to stage an open battle between the National Park Service and the Forest Service. Without any intent to wound your pride, I may say the Forester might not regard the dedication of another 300,000 acres of the Olympic National Forest to National Park purposes as nearly so serious as a defeat of the big objectives of sustained yield management toward which he is directing his efforts and in the attainment of which interdepartmental accord will be more effective than discord.[41]

Kneipp was referring to Chief Forester Silcox's efforts to implement the 1933 National Plan for American Forestry (the Copeland Report), which had recently been published.

It was becoming clear that Region Six and the Olympic Forest no longer had the complete support of the chief forester's office in their local struggle to stop the park movement. The Washington office would assist the field, but only so long as the larger national objectives of the Forest Service were not compromised.

The Wallgren Park Bill

Consideration of the Olympic controversy as a local or subnational issue by the Forest Service's Washington office was reinforced by Kneipp's earlier observation that the battle seemed to be confined to Washington State. In the city of Washington, D.C., Kneipp noted, both Secretary Ickes and Park Service Director Arno Cammerer had been conciliatory and reasonable. "The legislation necessary to accomplish the extension of the present National Monument and to give it National Park status has not yet been introduced and we have no certain knowledge that it will be."[42]

However, the Forest Service did not have long to wait. Congressman Wallgren, whose district included Port Angeles, was soon to respond to the proposal sent to him by that city's chamber of commerce in February.

After receiving an advance copy of the bill to be introduced by Wallgren, Associate Chief Forester E.A. Sherman wrote Congressman Martin F. Smith:

> It is true that the Olympic Mountains are of spectacular character and great scenic grandeur. Under National Forest management their inspirational and scenic qualities are being carefully conserved under plans which will make them fully useful to the people of the United States. The debatable question is that of placing under the National Park management large volumes of merchantable timber which normally would be subject to controlled industrial utilization.[43]

When the Wallgren bill (H.R. 7086, 74th Congress, 1st session) was introduced in April 1935, a copy was sent to the Portland regional office with a request for a report to the chief forester. Regional Forester Buck quickly responded, recommending that the monument be returned to national forest status so that it "may serve its greatest economic and social use." Again stressing that Forest Service administration of the monument was economical, that it would cost the Park Service much more to administer, and that the Forest Service was studying the elk problem and was capable of protecting them, Buck argued that sustained yield management of the area would result in far greater revenue to commerce. He continued:

> Recreation can be correlated with timber utilization . . . so as to yield practically the same revenues and enjoyment, and furnish a livelihood to as many people engaged in the recreational businesses as it would if reserved exclusively for recreational use. . . .

Past experience indicates that once a National Park is established within a National Forest area, there is constant agitation to enlarge the Park. In this case, such agitation had and would continue to upset the establishment of sustained yield cutting units, not only in the Forest but on adjacent state and private lands and would be a primary factor in preventing stabilization of the lumber industry in an area where 70% of the population depend on this industry for a livelihood and where a majority always will have to look to the manufacture of forest products for their employment.[44]

Buck attached a suggested letter (drafted by his office for the secretary's signature) from the secretary of agriculture to the secretary of the interior, in which he argued that:

Agitation to change the status of the basic resource of this region will prevent the formation of land use plans providing for stable community development. The removal of any amount of timber from the channels of commerce will materially affect the permanency of the industry and the commerce of the cities of Aberdeen, Hoquiam, Port Angeles, Port Townsend, and Shelton. These communities are still in a position to make land use plans so as to sustain their industries.[45]

Pulp and Paper to the Rescue

Buck's comments were based in part on an extensive 1935 study of the Grays Harbor area lumber industry by the Forest Service's Ira J. Mason. Mason wrote that all of the sawmills in the area were installed before 1920 and several of them were over forty years old. After reviewing the economy of local industries and communities from the standpoint of the Service's value orientation, he discussed the causes of the impending timber depletion predicted for the Grays Harbor area. He commented reprovingly:

Excessive sawmill installations have been made to liquidate "overstocking" of mature timber. Mills have been installed with no consideration of permanent timber supplies, but only as to a timber supply adequate to depreciate them. . . .

The end of the life span of the sawmill industry here is now in sight. That it will have extended for 60 years is not due to any planning on the part of the timber industry but rather to the huge original timber supply and the restrictions on production imposed by general market conditions. . . .

If cuts had been held down to 400 to 500 million feet annually . . . the industry would have been maintained on a permanent basis. It is obvious that if the industries and towns had grown at this conservative rate, there would be no problem of maintenance of various forms of social service and communications facilities which would have been established. . . . Too long a delay will result in abandoned mills and the decay of settlements.[46]

Mason and his fellow foresters wanted more of the hemlock timber currently left standing in the forests to be utilized. They regarded it as wasteful to let it remain or to burn it. Converting the hemlock and waste into paper pulp was seen as the answer. They felt that more paper mills were needed. Oddly, it seemed irrelevant to them that there was little or no market for paper pulp or hemlock. That hemlock was selling for about two dollars per thousand board feet and that Grays Harbor had excessive stocks of it apparently bore no importance. Mason wrote that there was "only one pulp mill located on Grays Harbor. This is difficult to understand."[47]

Grays Harbor civic leaders, aware that surplus raw material was available for pulping, followed up on Forest Service encouragement to attract pulp mills. W.C. Mumaw, manager of the Grays Harbor Special Industries Committee, informed Buck in October 1935 that his committee had four different financial groups interested in the establishment of a guaranteed supply of pulpwood for the mill investors. Later, noting that foreign competition was making the depressed market even more unstable, Mumaw commented: "You are aware, of course, of what is happening in Canada. American money has gone up there with an attempt to establish a large mill at Prince Rupert. This is all based on government grants but they are looking to the United States for the market for the pulp. If we could immediately establish several mills here I am sure we could get the markets that they propose to get."[48]

The market for pulp, particularly for newsprint, was perhaps even worse than either the Forest Service or the Grays Harbor interests knew. At the November meeting of a special Port Angeles Chamber of Commerce committee on newsprint, attended by Washington State Land Commissioner T.S. Goodyear, E.J. Hanzlik of the Forest Service, and other officials, it was disclosed that there was a great likelihood that American newsprint plants on the West Coast would either have to go out of business or be converted to manufacturing other materials. As the Forest Service had large amounts of pulp timber in the area, the committee concluded that this agency and the state of Washington could well take official action recommending restriction of newsprint imports into this country from Canada.[49]

T.T. Aldwell, chairman of the chamber's Industrial Committee, wrote to the new Olympic forest supervisor, J.R. Bruckart, a few days later describing the usurpation by Canada and other foreign countries of the American newsprint market. He noted that the present newsprint price of forty dollars per ton was far below the recognized production cost of forty-seven dollars per ton. Aldwell stated that if a quota or tariff were not established on the importation of newsprint, to permit existing plants to operate both at cost and at a reasonable percentage of their capacity, they would probably have to close down.[50]

Meanwhile Buck informed Mumaw and the Grays Harbor interests that, while no definite commitment of federal timber or pulp could be made for their proposed pulp mill, the Forest Service was "intensely interested" in securing cooperatively managed sustained yield units, which would tend to stabilize the industry. He suggested that new legislation might be needed before such joint public/private sustained yield units could be worked out.[51]

Two months later, Buck notified the chief forester that logging companies on the Olympic Peninsula faced a critical problem and that decisions were needed regarding what might be done with the timber on the Olympic National Forest to procure cooperatively managed sustained yield units. As he saw it, the problem facing the logging companies was that the private Douglas fir timber was about gone and the high percentage of hemlock in the remaining stands precluded an economic operation at the existing price for pulp species. Supplying Douglas fir logs from the national forest was thought an imperfect solution because they grew in long stringers that included high percentages of other unmarketable species. Excluding these species from cutting was described by the Forest Service as "uneconomic and poor forestry." On this basis, Buck requested assignment to Region Six of a Forest Service pulp specialist, B. Frank Heintzleman, to solve the problem of utilizing the pulp species and putting the local timber industry on a permanent basis.[52]

Heintzleman studied the situation and in March 1936 drew up a report called "A Discussion of Measures to Help Stabilize the Grays Harbor Region," in which he disclosed: "It is evident that some well-planned control should be established as soon as possible over the whole Grays Harbor timber situation. The extensive cut-over lands must be put to use growing future timber supplies if the community is to survive; an orderly shift of a large part of the timber use from lumber to pulp and paper must be effected; the average yearly production must be reduced to accord with the productive capacity of the region."[53]

Heintzleman proposed that if the Forest Service could get iron-clad assurances of adequate reforestation and proper handling and protection of private timberlands at Grays Harbor, then that agency would be in a position to allow overcutting of national forest timber during the "lean" period that would have to be faced before the forest on the cut-over lands reached merchantable size. He continued:

> It is impracticable to obtain satisfactory assurances for long-term good forestry practices from the hundreds of private owners in this region. Their holdings should be grouped for management purposes and the public agencies should have a strong voice in the management. . . .
>
> The setting up of a federally or state-controlled corporation under a federal or state granted charter, with the landowners exchanging title to their cut-over lands for stock certificates of the corporation, should be a good approach to the problem. The corporation's lands could then be considered as a part of a joint sustained yield working circle which includes public virgin timber. . . . The output from the working circle would be allocated to a specified community but not an individual concern . . . the only change from existing [timber] sale conditions being the restriction on the locality where the material is to be manufactured. . . .
>
> The charter should provide that . . . the government would have a controlling voice in the establishment and direction of corporation policies.[54]

Heintzleman listed several of what he considered less desirable alternatives for stabilizing the region's communities and industries, one of which, the "Joint Sustained Yield Management Unit," finally became established on a smaller scale through the passage of the Sustained-Yield Forest Management Act (58 Stat. 132) in 1944.[55]

The Controversy Continues

While Mason's, Buck's, and Heintzleman's sustained yield community stabilization ideas were being formulated, the park controversy continued. The elk still posed an unsolved problem when Murie of the Biological Survey completed his 1935 study for the Forest Service. He recommended purchase of the small ranches blocking elk migration, increased lowland stocking of elk, and limited hunting each year.[56]

The Forest Service field staff planned a new elk hunt for the fall in cooperation with the State Game Department. However, upon finding out about his staff's recommendation, Buck countermanded their decisions and ordered their letters recalled. He later advised Washington that because of the complications of administrative jurisdiction in the Olympic forest and monument, no hunt would be held that fall. "It is generally agreed by local [public] organizations—the Biological Survey, the Forest Service, and State men—that there is actually an excess number of elk on certain drainages of the West Side and that the excess should be controlled, but now is not the opportune time to do the work."[57]

The Park Service itself was not idle. It was busily preparing a motion picture on the Olympics to be shown in the East that coming winter.[58] Also, Acting Director Arthur Demeray had written several letters in which he sought to discredit the Forest Service's sustained yield ideas. In a letter to Mathias of the Hoquiam Rotary Club, Demeray observed: "It is hard to understand at this time why the entire economic stability of the Peninsula should be hitched to a small virgin forest."[59] In another letter Demeray commented that sustained yield was only an unfulfilled promise. Assistant Regional Forester Horton, who had obtained copies of the letters, inquired angrily of Kneipp: "Isn't the NPS getting off their reservation? Can't we do anything about it?"[60]

Horton, who had secured a newspaper clipping of some of the same material that appeared in Demeray's letters, confided to Kneipp: "Now they are publishing their stuff. I would expect to be separated from the Service if I ever wrote a similar letter regarding the NPS. Since this is in public print do we continue to allow them to swing on us? Truly, we are the Carnera of Government Bureaus. We just stand and take it."[61]

Kneipp answered that he had prepared a letter for Chief Silcox to answer Demeray, but Silcox had concluded that response was poor strategy. Kneipp reminded Horton of the quotation, "O that mine enemy would write a book," and added that he doubted the possibility of the Wallgren bill passing during the current congressional session. "In 1936 things may be different."[62] Kneipp's prediction proved to be correct, for there was only minor sparring as each side continued to press its case with the local population for the rest of the year.

The Reorganization Threat

Other pressures were beginning to bear upon the Forest Service. The battle over bureau reorganization was heating up again. In a December 1935 letter to the regional forester, Olympic Supervisor Bruckart described a recent meeting with Congressman Wesley Lloyd in Tacoma regarding both the Olympic park proposal and the Lewis bill, which proposed transfer of the Forest Service to the Department of the Interior. He reported discussing with Lloyd the disadvantages of such a transfer, pointing out the Service's close association with the other scientific bureaus in the Department of Agriculture. Regretting that his time with the congressman had been too short "to outline the objectionable features of the park bill," Bruckart noted that he planned to send him some basic facts and data. His letter concluded: "I plan to work out a line of contact with Lloyd through someone in his district to whom he looks for counsel and advice and will take up through them forestry matters which should be brought to Mr. Lloyd's attention."[63]

Bruckart had evidently been contacting or planning to contact several of the members of the Washington congressional delegation, because attached to the memorandum quoted above were forms to be used for analyzing and classifying the attitudes and personality characteristics of certain key individuals. Captions, like "Attitudes towards F.S.," "Attitudes towards pending legislation," "Whom does he look to for counsel," "Who in the F.S. knows him best," "Who this man counsels in Washington, D.C.," and "Hobbies, interests, etc. which would facilitate contact," were listed on the forms with blank spaces between them. A handwritten note containing some of this information on Congressman Wallgren was attached to this same memorandum. One of the notations read: "Mr. Wallgren is interested in conservation and while he might be classified as a sentimentalist when it comes to the preservation of the forests, this is in some measure due to a lack of understanding of what the objectives of Forestry [are]."[64]

While Bruckart was apparently willing to become personally involved in the details of the Forest Service's political efforts, he did not feel his staff should do so. When a district ranger suggested presenting facts to local organizations to counter the forestry "mis-information" being circulated by Chris Morgenroth, a former forest ranger, now propark, Bruckart responded: "I am rather reluctant to advise any forest officer to actively engage in opposing the Wallgren Bill. We are prepared to furnish all persons interested in this proposal with facts and figures as to the real situation." He added that the public would be reached by a committee of interested persons formed by various peninsula communities to combat the bill. On another occasion, when a young junior forester on his staff asked Bruckart why the Forest Service didn't actively speak out against the Park Service misinformation, the supervisor responded, "You don't lobby or take part in politics."[65]

In January 1936, Plumb, now an assistant regional forester in Portland, made a trip to the Olympic Peninsula. He reported that the Port Angeles Chamber of Commerce had reversed its support of a park and had decided to drop the question entirely. This development did not stop aggressive community action, however. He noted that petitions were being circulated, Morgenroth had been speaking to the women's clubs in favor of the park, and someone had sponsored a propark essay contest in the schools with a prize of twenty-five dollars. Meanwhile in Shelton representatives from Hoquiam, Aberdeen, Shelton, Port Townsend, Sequim, and Hoodsport had met to discuss ways of fighting the inclusion of an additional seventeen billion board feet of timber in the park. Plumb noted that Supervisor Bruckart attended this meeting and would advise the region of its outcome. He said there were local reports that the Wallgren bill would come out of committee on February 3 and a hearing would be held on the eleventh. Plumb asked his staff: Can our Washington Office confirm? . . . It is my feeling that the subject is of so much concern from the economic standpoint and from the future forestry standpoint that someone thoroughly conversant with the details should be present at the hearing." He added he had heard gossip that Major O.A. Tomlinson of the Park Service was going east to the hearings.[66]

Actually, Tomlinson went east to show his agency's Olympic film at the 1936 Conference on National Parks sponsored by the American Planning and Civic Association. Later, when the association invited Chief Forester Silcox to view the film and comment on it, Silcox was out of town. This type of publicity was successful in arousing influential persons, however, and may have been partly responsible for the sudden direct involvement of President Roosevelt in the controversy.

The Letters-to-the-President Episode

On February 18, 1936, President Roosevelt sent a memorandum on the Mount Olympus National Monument to the Agriculture and Interior secretaries, saying:

> I understand that there is a forest area immediately adjacent to the national monument. Why should two Departments run this

acreage? If the forest portion is not to be used for eventual commercial forestation and cutting why not include the forest area in the national monument?

This is a matter which should be settled by Mr. Silcox and Mr. Cammerer.

Please let me have a report recommending executive action.[67]

This memorandum seems to refer to the Olympic Primitive Area managed by the Forest Service along the east side of the national monument, which was scheduled for future logging. The Forest Service drafted an extensive reply to the president for the secretary of agriculture's signature. This letter avoided any mention of both the Olympic Primitive Area and the recent internal Forest Service proposal to enlarge it. In notes attached to the draft, E.E. Carter, a member of the chief forester's staff, commented: "This [draft] is silent about the proposed [enlarged] Primitive Area as [a] constructive alternative. This was purposely done and I think wisely so."[68]

This initial draft of the response to the president openly betrayed the value orientation of the Forest Service. It began: "The fundamental issue here is—to what extent can and should the basic economy of the Olympic Peninsula be crippled by withdrawing timber—upon which 90% of its population is now directly and indirectly dependent and upon which 96% can in the future be supported under sustained yield management—from economic use?"[69] The letter went on to describe how the national park plan proposed in the Wallgren bill would deprive 19,400 persons of a livelihood, while the Forest Service plan for protecting the Olympic scene would affect only 4,000 people. The Forest Service plan was stated to offer protection to virgin timber along many miles of existing and proposed travel routes. This was important, the letter said, because more than ninety percent of all mountain recreationists travel the automobile roads. "The plan here proposed is essentially that so successful in the White Mountain National Forest. . . . [It] has for years permitted dependent sawmills to run, with operations so screened that they do not interfere with heavy recreational travel and use."[70]

The letter reiterated how many more people would be left to shift for themselves under the park plan, and then stated that "without economic use of natural resources, dependent communities cannot enjoy those virgin timber areas. . . . From the standpoint of longtime public policy, economic use should be permitted. . . . For this is the policy which will make for development of communities and of the nation." The missive concluded by urging that authority be obtained for the president to retransfer jurisdiction over the Mount Olympus

National Monument and all other national monuments located within national forests back to the Department of Agriculture.[71]

Chief Forester Silcox and Agriculture Secretary Henry Wallace saw the president about the Olympic controversy on March 9, after the chief had conferred with the secretary. Following this meeting, the Forest Service decided not to send the first letter, but to draft another. One can infer from a comparison of the two letters that a decidedly propreservation tone was set by the president at that meeting. The new letter referred to six billion feet of virgin timber to be preserved under the Forest Service plan, rather than the four and one-half billion mentioned in the first letter; also it cautioned: "Adequate provision must be made for planned bread and butter uses of natural resources, else living standards will not permit that nationwide use and enjoyment of reserved virgin timber areas for which both the Forest Service and the Park Service are now planning." The letter went on to argue that a principle of managed land use was involved which was vital to the future social and economic welfare of the whole country.[72]

In an about-face from the earlier approach of deliberately avoiding mention of the Olympic Forest Primitive Area, the second letter brought out the administrative actions being taken to safeguard the recreational and aesthetic values in the 247,000 acres of land adjacent to the Mount Olympus National Monument, a region containing nearly three billion feet of virgin timber. The revised draft to the president concluded:

> This will create no legal or physical obstacle to transfer of jurisdiction later. . . .
> In view of the conference with you, and of the values, principles, and matters of policy which are involved, I urge that this Olympic matter be left for the present as it now stands excepting only for this Department's administrative action which, based on careful examinations which have extended over many years, will assure added protection to recreation and aesthetic values.[73]

This draft was the subject of a conference between Chief Silcox and Secretary Wallace on March 17, 1936. After this interview, Silcox's special assistant wrote: "Upon his return to the office, Mr. Silcox stated that it had been decided that, in view of the situation as it developed at the White House, no written reply to the President's memorandum of February 18 need now be made."[74] The secretary did ask the chief forester to continue conferences with Park Service Director Arno Cammerer about the Olympic situation.

The Primitive Area Enlargement

In December the Wilderness Society had written letters to Silcox and Cammerer stating that, before deciding whether to support the Wallgren bill, the organization was anxious to learn what guarantees each agency would make to protect wilderness values in the Olympics. The society asked for detailed statements about roads, cabins, mining, water power, and even the reservation of trails from the upper Queets and Bogachiel River valleys.[75]

The Forest Service waited to respond until March, when the episode with the president was over, then informed the society of its plan to enlarge the primitive area. At the same time the agency reiterated most of the arguments and value positions used in the draft letters, such as recommending wide use of resources to maintain living standards. "The park would . . . cut the economic heart out of a wonderfully productive forest area," the agency wrote, "which, though relatively small, is of national significance in that it contains 2.4% of all the commercially merchantable timber left in the entire continental United States." The same dependency figures were cited. The letter went on:

> Qualified men have made detailed studies on the ground of the economic situation and of the physical aspects of recreational and aesthetic values. They have kept in touch with local and national developments and trends. And the whole thing has been reviewed, during the last two months, by Regional representatives in collaboration with members of Mr. Silcox's own staff.
>
> All this has been done because we feel that this Olympic situation is tremendously important. It involves a basic issue, a principle of managed land use, which is vital to the social and economic welfare of the whole country. . . . the Forest Service plan [an increase in the size of the existing primitive area] would protect from commercial use almost three billion feet of virgin timber on some 246,000 acres . . . in addition to the three billion feet on some 290-odd thousand acres in the Monument which, as you know, was created at the request of the Forest Service[76] and was protected and administered by it for some twenty-eight years. . . .
>
> Until jurisdictional decision on this Olympic situation is reached, the Forest Service believes such immediate administrative action should be taken as will . . . give added assurance to

the public that major recreational and aesthetic values will be safeguarded. . . .

This will, we feel, provide safeguards directly comparable to those provided by National Monument or National Park status.[77]

The Forest Service then indicated that its primitive area expansion plan included a road into Seven Lakes Basin and a transmountain road across the area. "Years of study of the conditions on the ground convince us that these two roads will add to the opportunity to use the area properly." The Service also planned to permit mining and to place trails for fire protection along all the main streams.[78]

In spite of the official announcement of the enlarged primitive area, the Wilderness Society opted to support the national park bill because the Park Service gave assurances of a larger wilderness area and met all the society's conditions on roadless, trailless, and miningless areas.[79]

The Forest Service publicly issued its plan for the enlarged primitive area on April 14, 1936. The introductory statement of this report, about 1½ pages in length, concentrated on the importance of the lumber industry, the "shortage" of timber, and the consequent closing of sawmills. No mention was made of recreation or aesthetic values. High-yield forestry and forest management could support 100,000 people, the report maintained.[80]

Although Regional Forester Buck, apparently in response to the Wallgren bill, had planned some enlargement of the primitive area as early as January, the president's intervention had motivated Assistant Chief Forester Granger to order a much larger increase containing more old growth virgin timber. This increase did not please the regional or forest staffs, and Assistant Regional Forester Horton commented unenthusiastically on the primitive area report: "It will appear rather peculiar in some instances as to policy, but the Chief has requested it in about the form now set up."[81]

With the House Public Lands Committee hearings on the Wallgren bill about to begin, the revised primitive area did not receive widespread publicity until later. Bruckart distributed forty-one copies of the report to various influential persons in mid-September. The secretary of agriculture issued his formal approval of the primitive area in July (after Congress adjourned for the summer without passing the Wallgren bill). Kneipp asked Buck to make sure the secretary's approval received wide newspaper distribution.[82]

Protection to the wilderness afforded by the primitive area was apparently not considered permanent by the field levels of the Forest Service. A second report by Heintzleman included all of the commercial timber in the primitive area in three of the working circles that he had developed concurrently with the planning for the enlargement of the primitive area.[83]

Summary

The "last ditch" retreat by the Forest Service into enlargement of the Olympic Primitive Area was obviously a consolidative decision. With its domain and authority severely threatened by presidential power, the agency finally sought to preserve its jurisdiction in the Olympics by revising and re-ordering its plans and programs. This was clearly a reluctant move for the foresters, who throughout most of the three-year struggle had attempted to control the forces of change in their environment by reemphasizing traditional values and premises. Most evident was their focus on telic forestry, the utilitarian value that the primary purpose of national forests is to stabilize and maintain local forest industries and communities. The Service was willing to go to great lengths to assert its "correct" views, but the alternative approach of disarming the opposition by anticipating the forces of change, of promoting enlargement of the primitive area before those forces became organized and overt, did not find favor.

5

The Park Campaign Triumphs: April 1936 Through February 1938

The primitive area enlargement was in fact too late to provide a viable alternative to the demands for a park. Washington's Congressman Monrad Wallgren, who had introduced his park bill the year before, continued to press for the reintroduced bill. Relatively certain that most of his constituency now favored a park, Wallgren persuaded the chairman of the House Public Lands Committee to hold hearings on the bill. The hearings were long and sometimes acrimonious, and the Forest Service did not win much support from the committee for its views on the values of telic forestry and timber primacy. The elk and recreation issues merged briefly and disappeared into the polarized larger issue of national park versus national forest. However, the untimely scheduling of two additional elk hunts during this period revived the elk issue once again, to the detriment of the Forest Service's political position.

Two major factors appeared: a lack of support for the Forest Service from the secretary of agriculture's office and the personal intervention, again, of the president in favor of a park. In spite of these obstacles, the Forest Service fought the park to the end. In a final effort, it once again took a consolidative position in order to protect its domain. Again, the change came too late, and defeat ensued.

The Hearings

The Forest Service had continued to present its point of view at chamber of commerce assemblies and at meetings of the State Planning Council and of the Olympic Development League. The league especially "was used to help us talk about and explain the situation," according to Assistant Regional Forester Plumb. "The Park Service brought out propaganda bulletins that were absolutely wrong," Plumb continued, "but the Forest Service didn't do enough to counter them. I went out on my own time to give the facts."[1]

The Forest Service did seek to counter propark articles and editorials such as those in *Nature* magazine and the *New York Herald Tribune*. They also took advantage of information requests from Congressman Martin F. Smith to have additional materials passed through him to the Public Lands Committee of the House of Representatives. The chief forester's special assistant, R.F. Hammatt, noted: "Since Congressman Smith had asked for information, we are at liberty to give it."[2] Apparently, Forest Service personnel in the nation's capital felt more reluctant to initiate contact with congressmen than did field personnel like Olympic Supervisor Bruckart and Regional Forester Buck.

When Hammatt informed Buck about the forthcoming House Public Lands Committee hearings on the Wallgren bill, Buck responded:

> Congressman Smith has been working very hard against the Wallgren Bill for many months. . . . I have discussed the matter with him and he has cooperated closely with people interested in killing the bill. . . . We have known about the scheduled hearing for some time and have done considerable work out here at this end with the local people in connection with building up proper representation from local interests in the hearing. . . . P.S. I have just learned by phone that Asahel Curtis leaves tonight for Washington to appear at the hearing. . . . He is a staunch friend of the Forest Service. . . . I am very glad we have been able to work this out. . . .

Assistant Regional Forester Horton suggested to Bruckart that "since there will be discussion of this whole Olympic National Park matter in Congress and other places, I believe you should discuss [the primitive area enlargement of 1936] with your key men, particularly in the Grays Harbor country, in order that they may be informed of what is going on before they read about it in the newspapers."[3]

The committee hearings on the "Bill to Establish the Mount Olympus National Park in the State of Washington" (H.R. 7086) began on April 23, 1936. They continued for nine days, with public and private organizations on both sides of the issue testifying. The Park Service was represented by Cammerer and the Forest Service by Kneipp, who was aided by Assistant Regional Forester Plumb. Neither Chief Forester Silcox nor Secretary of Agriculture Wallace testified, although Secretary of the Interior Ickes and former Park Service Director Horace Albright did, both making strong attacks upon the Forest Service.

Ickes singled out Plumb with statements such as "I am afraid that as an economist, Forest Supervisor Plumb is a good lumberman."[4]

Various persons and private organizations also testified both for and against the park proposal; the transcribed testimony filled close to 300 pages. Before the committee Kneipp denounced the public relations efforts of the Park Service in advocating a park on the Olympic Peninsula. He attacked Director Cammerer's statements depicting the Forest Service as exploiters versus the Park Service as conservationists, and he explained that "the real issue is the economic security of some 75,000 people."

> The major resource for the creative use of the local labor on that peninsula is the timber. . . . Seventy percent of the total payroll . . . is represented by lumber industries.
>
> . . . You will see a lot of country that has been cut over. . . . it will be some time and it will require considerable effort before it again becomes fully productive. There was some question in the minds of the owners of that land as to whether that expenditure of time and effort would be justified, because it would indicate a hiatus between the utilization of the present stand and the new stand, but it was pointed out that if the remaining timber was properly handled it will carry the industry for a sufficient period of time to permit a reforestation of the cut-over lands so that by that time you can pick up again on those lands and have a continuous and permanent production of timber—a permanent industry.[5]

Kneipp said that the Forest Service had not pressed the sale of national forest timber—and obtained larger receipts for the U.S. Treasury—because that "would have just simply complicated an already acute condition in that very territory where the private owners are liquidating in a noneconomic and deplorable way even under present conditions."[6]

One question addressed to Plumb by Congressman Compton I. White brought out a curious reversal of the dependency situation. Asked, first, if the Forest Service's program for development and sustained yield in the area of the proposed park relied on the Grays Harbor mills as a market outlet and, second, if the failure of these firms would "be very detrimental to the Forest Service . . . in carrying out their plans," Plumb responded affirmatively. "If the industry at Grays Harbor folded up we would not have a market for part of the timber."[7]

Kneipp concluded the Forest Service's primary testimony:

There is not much else to be said. This forest has been administered by the Forest Service since 1905, not without error, of course, because the whole thing was a grouping, as a part of a very radical readjustment of standards and practices. But, as that Olympic Forest stands today, it is beautiful and it is protected and there are definite plans for its permanent protection and at the same time, it is an integration of economic activity and life and there has been until recently, only a single agency of administration which is most economic. Why should it be changed?[8]

Secretary Ickes then summarized the views of the park proponents: "I should like to make this point: sustained-yield logging, multiple use, or any of the smooth-sounding techniques of the Forest Service are no substitute for a national park, and will not save an area of national park quality. Neither will they replace trees that are centuries old after they once have been cut down."[9]

Early in June special action was taken by Representative Arthur Greenwood of the House Rules Committee, apparently at Ickes's instigation, to provide rapid consideration of the Wallgren bill by the House of Representatives and to limit debate to one hour.[10] Despite this move, the Mount Olympus park bill failed to pass before Congress adjourned for the summer of 1936.[11]

The committee hearings, however, had a considerable effect on the residents of the Olympic Peninsula and surrounding areas. Plumb attended a meeting of the Olympic Peninsula Development League in early June and found that there had been a decided change of heart among the people of some of the communities. They apparently now felt that a park was inevitable and that it should be confined to as small an area as possible. "I suspect it is through the influence of local representatives," Plumb wrote in a memo to the files. Seemingly writing an apologia, he continued:

The proponents of the bill in Washington, D.C. took more time for preparation for the hearing on the bill and had more time before the Committee at Washington than the opponents had. . . . [The] Park Service had their data in excellent shape from several months work on the Peninsula. . . . The Forest Service representatives did not have the time to prepare an adequate case. It would seem desirable to make plans now for an aggressive campaign, to get the facts before the people so that an intelligent solution of the problem may be made.[12]

Preparation for the Next Round

Plumb's suggestion of an aggressive campaign did not take hold in Washington until mid-September 1936, when the chief forester's special assistant, R.F. Hammatt, advised Regional Forester Buck and his assistant, F.M. Brundage, to make several strategic moves in preparing for more Olympic park hearings. Hammatt wrote:

> Perhaps Alex Bailee of the Rainier Park Association can carry protests from local organizations at the next hearings. . . . Get the F.S. Neiholm statement regarding Grant of the Park Service. I hate to use stuff like this, but we should have it in reserve. . . .
>
> Get out the Wallgren statement made at the public meeting in Port Angeles favoring a *developed* Park (use to sway eastern pro-primitive area people). . . .
>
> Get Harry LaGear of Port Angeles to get a petition signed by a great number of responsible people in Port Angeles. It might be convincingly used against Port Angeles' statement of "solid" position for a Park.
>
> We need carefully prepared material, including photographs.[13]

Forethought on strategy for further hearings on a reintroduced Mount Olympus national park bill continued on the Washington office level. C.M. Granger, now an assistant chief forester, thought that a concise statement of the Forest Service's position, featuring their "constructive plan for handling the Primitive Area and catching up all the loose ends of our first presentation," was needed.[14]

Hammatt displayed the most politically astute approach. Having traveled to the Olympic Peninsula that summer, returning with a detailed battle plan and well aware of Congressman Wallgren's reelection campaign promises to reintroduce the park bill, Hammatt observed that national park proponents were still actively canvassing the peninsula and were holding out the lure of increased tourism. He commented that this group now had "the confidence that breeds confidence; they feel that the fight is 'in the bag,' that the Olympics will be the stepping-stone to King's Canyon, Jackson Hole, Diamond Lake, Rocky Mountain, and a host of other additions from National Forests. The Olympics *is* 'in the bag' for a Park unless the Forest Service and the Department do more than just continue their opposition."[15]

Hammatt was very thorough and quite optimistic. He knew how individual Congressmen were leaning and why. He argued:

To win, we must have thorough preparation and Eastern as well as local support, and must put on a real show before the Public Lands Committee. At those hearings the Secretary should lead off, in person. He might recall the Department's long jurisdiction over the entire area; our intimate study and knowledge of its resources. . . .

Our presentation must be snappy and interesting. . . . It should be graphic, with each individual exhibit painting one instantly grasped picture. It must . . . present both economic and recreational angles.[16]

Hammatt's enthusiasm was contagious; the Region Six personnel began to organize their case again. Rudo L. Fromme, former Olympic Forest supervisor, was assigned from the regional office to do a "sustained yield study" on the Olympic Peninsula.[17] Actually, Fromme was charged with preparing detailed physical and economic material for the anticipated hearings; he was also to make contacts with the labor unions and, after a "build-up," to see that the unions let senators Homer Bone and Lewis Schwellenbach of Washington State know their position. Assistant Regional Forester F.V. Horton noted that Fromme was spending two weeks in the field and then a few days in the regional office before going out again.

Horton was also concerned about the position of the Zellerbach interests. He asked Associate Chief Forester Earle Clapp to give him "an angle" on them because their "local men say they will fight a Park, but in Port Angeles they are supporting it or at least not fighting." Horton wrote to Clapp:

Frankland contacted head of holding company (power) from the South. . . . Says he controls 16 companies and will go to bat when we say go. Will work on representation from the South. Have a fine contact with J.D. Ross, [who] says if a bill passes he will personally make a trip and ask President to veto. In meantime, is doing his bit.[18]

Assistant Chief Forester Kneipp responded for Clapp with several points of strategic advice, both on Horton's observations and his accompanying outline of their battle plans. His reply concluded:

The foregoing are the only points that have excited any mental reaction other than one of appreciation. Otherwise, the planned approach to the problem seems logical and complete. Of course, I have no doubt that you will get better as you go along so that when the new bill is introduced, the oratorical, statistical, photographic, graphic, and textural presentations will mark a new era in effective legislative procedure.[19]

Kneipp was trying to stimulate a thorough, competent effort on the part of the regional staff, as the Washington office had its time occupied with other problems. Commenting earlier on the previous congressional hearing, he had noted that "the graphic and economic data presented by the National Park Service were far superior to those offered by the Forest Service as to make rather a pathetic comparison."[20]

Unanticipated Problems Develop

Several events then occurred to undermine the Forest Service's position. First, the Washington State Planning Council came out in favor of a compromise park considerably smaller than that prescribed by the original Wallgren bill. Excluded from this proposal were a number of areas that local groups wanted kept out of the park. Concerned about the council's defusing action, Kneipp wrote to Horton: "These revised boundaries are going to make it harder to rally a support of continuation of the Forest Service plan of management. . . . Your local Peninsula leaders may recognize the new lines as acceptable, making it difficult [for us] to explain away the supportive public sentiment."[21]

The next disturbing event was the opening of elk season by the state on the west side of the Olympics. Two hundred and seventy-five elk were killed in the twelve-day season, 100 to 110 of these in the Hoh drainage. Many carcasses were left unclaimed, and a conservative estimate was that twenty to thirty percent of the meat spoiled.[22] Supervisor Bruckart informed the regional forester that certain Aberdeen interests were protesting the opening of elk season and that some Park Service employees were roving the state speaking out against the hunting of elk on the Peninsula, stating that for every elk taken legally, seven to ten elk were killed illegally each year.[23] Thus, public sentiment against Forest Service efforts to scientifically manage the elk was again aroused.

The third blow to the Forest Service's revived momentum to "stop the park" came when Congressman Wallgren was interviewed after his reelection. Wallgren opined that no further congressional hearings would be scheduled on his new park bill because the previous hearing had been so detailed and complete that its repetition was unnecessary.[24]

Shortly thereafter, in a report to the chief forester on the State Planning Council's new park proposal, Region Six described the amount of timber lost to such a park and its impact on the economy. After reading this, Kneipp commented to Hammatt that, while the majority of points were undoubtedly correct, he questioned the volume of commercial timber listed within the revised boundaries and its social and economic significance stated in the report. He observed that "it seems mistaken strategy to include the timber within the present Monument in our estimates of potential industrial use and employment. Such statements would be used against us as indications that if the national monument were restored to our jurisdiction we would allow commercial exploitation of the timber."[25]

This apparently was the first close reading Kneipp had given the data being forwarded, as such timber volumes from the monument and the primitive area had consistently been included in past working circles of timber management plans and in the various dependency projections. Kneipp concluded that this particular statement from the region was weak and not convincing; it did not persuasively demonstrate that creation of the proposed park would markedly increase the difficulty or the cost of administering the remaining national forest lands, or that it would have any early adverse effects upon industry, employment, or cash returns to the counties.

Kneipp was now convinced that the new State Planning Council proposal for a small park had completely undermined the logic of the Forest Service's previous "proper land management" arguments. He explained to Buck that the chief objections to the park proposed by the council must now be based on points of principle rather than on major adverse consequences of an economic, industrial, or administrative character. He suggested that Buck stress the shortcomings of dual administration, portraying it as unnecessarily expensive and as creating needless problems of coordination and imposing on the public the need to deal with two agencies when one would suffice. "However," he wrote, "this premise is based upon the idea that administration of the Monument otherwise will be restored to the Forest Service. If the Monument is to be permanently administered by the National Park Service there is little weight to the above objections."[26]

Indeed, former Chief Forester Graves agreed. In a letter dated December 19, 1936, to Forest Service Information Chief H.A. Smith, Graves, now dean of forestry at Yale University, said that the Service's approach to sustained yield in the Olympics was faulty and that the interbureau conflict was going to result in a big park. He suggested that the Forest Service "recognize the special character of the Olympic problem and ask for legislation to lock up certain portions as primitive areas. It is only by some such device that the public will be assured that the timber will not be opened up by some later administration."[27]

Even more depressing to the Washington office staff in their new efforts to fight the Wallgren bill was the report given them by pulp specialist B. Frank Heintzleman, who had recently returned to Washington, D.C., from the West. Having completed a year of work on the development of a large pulp industry on the Olympic Peninsula, he told the Washington office staff that public sentiment on the peninsula was positively and preponderantly in favor of the dedication of the Olympic area to exclusive recreational uses. He also reported that resistance by the Forest Service would not only be futile but would engender antagonisms detrimental to other important objectives. At the same time, Heintzleman agreed that the Forest Service might emphasize the inadvisability of dual administration of intimately related lands. He also supported Graves's view that substituting permanent legislative status for the primitive area and monument was a necessary Forest Service concession.[28]

Concluding that Heintzleman was right about public sentiment, Regional Forester Buck argued:

> Undoubtedly local public sentiment is for a National Park in the Olympics. There is some support in other parts of the state. A large part of the people are passive, but there is no aggressive group opposing the creation of a park. . . .
>
> A change in our attitude now will do no more than make certain of a National Park. To follow procedure outlined by Heintzleman might even result in all our Primitive Areas being made Parks. . . .
>
> . . . should we agree that any area be given legal status by Act of Congress, we are under the situation now existing, agreeing to the creation of a national park. . . . there has been created a lack of confidence in the Forest Service.

Buck felt the Service should wholeheartedly and consistently adhere to its present stand based on a principle of land management; otherwise, they should completely abandon it.[29]

Buck's comments were passed on to six high-level staff members by Assistant Chief Kneipp. C.M. Granger, Earl Loveridge, and Associate Chief Earle Clapp agreed with the regional forester; Earl Tinker and Special Assistant Hammatt seemed to think that "something was wrong with this picture" and that the Forest Service hadn't "sold" its position to the public on the Olympics; and Chief Forester Ferdinand

Silcox and Kneipp himself evidently didn't concur, for two weeks later the chief proposed a compromise plan to the secretary of agriculture. Silcox pointed out that even though Congressman Wallgren's new park bill excluded six billion board feet of timber from that included in the former bill, eight billion board feet would still remain within the park. He suggested to Secretary Wallace that the position of the department should be to

> 1) Present the factors showing that it is most effective and efficient for the Forest Service to administer the Monument as part of the Olympic National Forest, 2) Stress the Forest Service's Recreation Plan for a Primitive-type area as opposed to the intensive development likely to come from a Park, 3) The area should have a formal dedication by the Secretary along the same lines as the adjacent National Forest Primitive Area approved by Wallace on July 3, 1936.
>
> If this course is unacceptable to Congress and a National Park is inevitable, then we should place the full support of the Department back of the boundaries recommended in the Proposal of the Washington State Planning Council.

Silcox thought this smaller park would provide "adequate samples" of the big timber stands which typify the Olympic Peninsula. He concluded that if Congress should reject the boundaries proposed by the Washington State Planning Council as inadequate, the department should "exhaust every effort to induce Congressional acceptance of boundaries which will exclude the merchantable timber resources from the proposed Park to the fullest degree practicable."[30]

Kneipp informed Buck of the chief forester's proposals and noted that although the secretary of agriculture had been unwilling to intervene personally in the park controversy last spring, he might now be willing to do so. Kneipp also encouraged Horton and Buck to do a better public relations job:

> The success the Park proponents are meeting with the garden clubs in Washington State causes one to wonder whether you and C.J. are losing your principal appeal. Your statement that you have very little chance is quite disturbing. I thought the Forest Service also had motion pictures and qualified lecturers who are adept in creating public understanding of our work and purpose. . . . [Your] position seems to be that we should either stand pat or surrender. However, the majority [here] . . . feel compromise is not impracticable.[31]

The Second Wallgren Bill

When the new Wallgren bill (H.R. 4724, 75th Congress, 1st session) was introduced on February 15, 1937, Kneipp asked the clerk of the House Committee on Public Lands as to their intentions in regard to new hearings on the bill. While it was too early for definite plans, the clerk told him that because of the exhaustive sessions in 1936, further hearings were not believed necessary. When Kneipp suggested that there were many material changes in the new bill, the clerk indicated that perhaps a single-session hearing during one forenoon could be provided. Kneipp felt this was quite important, even if the Forest Service could only file a written statement, as it was viewed the sole means available to the Service for reaching the membership of the House of Representatives. Kneipp was afraid the new bill's deletion of six billion feet of timber adjacent to Grays Harbor might eliminate Congressman Smith's objections to the park.[32]

At the field level of the Forest Service, preparations against the anticipated Wallgren bill began. It was understood that the new bill would be similar to the park recommendations of the Washington State Planning Council. Seeking official state endorsement of the Planning Council's version, Senator Joseph L. Keeler, from the north end of the Olympic Peninsula, authored a memorial recommending this plan to Congress; the state senate passed it. Rudo Fromme, still working as a special antipark public relations officer for the regional office, visited Olympia to try to block passage of the memorial. He failed to persuade Ralph Metcalf, a state senator and the chairman of the senate's memorials committee, shortly before the full senate passed it; he then contacted several other legislators in an effort to have the memorial held in a house committee. Maps and notes were given to former State Legislator Tim Healey as ammunition in trying to influence three committee members whom Healey knew. Fromme also obtained a protest resolution from the State Sportsmen's Council against the Keeler memorial, and he found some antipark dissidents within The Seattle Mountaineers. During this time, Olympic Forest Supervisor Bruckart was amassing data and arguments for the chief's office to use in any new hearings.[33]

Bruckart's data and arguments were incorporated by the regional office into timber and recreation statements on House Bill 4724; these were forwarded to Washington, D.C.[34] The suggested timber statement included several of the value positions previously adopted by the Forest Service; the statement's summary contained the following positions:

1. The timber included in the Wallgren extension is of vital importance to the future industrial and social life of not only the Olympic Peninsula but of the entire west side of the State.
2. The future welfare of one million people in Western Washington depends primarily on the forest industries.
3. Every billion board feet of National Forest timber is of several times its value in influence in a forestry program to stabilize and maintain payrolls, homes, and the livelihood of people in Western Washington, or anywhere else the National Forests contain usable timber.
4. Private Douglas-fir and cedar timber supplies in the area are threatened with complete depletion in 12 years and private pulp stands of merchantable size in an additional 14 years. Cooperative management with the regulating influence of important bodies of National Forest timber is the more evident means of stabilizing the hurried and wasteful liquidation of private timber and for bringing about more efficient management of cutover lands. Every billion board feet impairs Federal influence in effecting a remedy.
5. Log imports cannot be expected to supply but little of the industrial needs of the Area.[35]

In another antipark effort, the Region Six office discussed the mineral tie-up question with the Army Corps of Engineers. With manganese classified as a war material, the engineers had intended to survey manganese deposits in the Olympic Mountains the next summer. Assistant Regional Forester Horton met with Colonel Robins of the corps to persuade him to request that the Wallgren bill be referred to the War Department because of the possible tie-up of manganese. Horton speculated that the War Department could well introduce a delay of at least a year until the survey was completed. After leaving Colonel Robins, Horton wrote Kneipp again: "Two notes from me today. Just saw Col. Robins. He has a chill in his pedal extremities. Frankly he is afraid of Harold [Ickes]. So am I."[36]

The Forest Service's fears of not having another hearing on the Wallgren bill were somewhat relieved when Clarence D. Martin, governor of Washington, requested the hearing. Silcox notified the Washington State Planning Council that the Forest Service was very gratified by the governor's action. He continued: "Fundamentally, the issue involved is one of social and resource planning, which inspires the hope that if the State of Washington is to be represented at the hearing its representative (other than the Governor personally) shall be one who is thoroughly conversant with the work of the State Planning Council and competent to discuss the issue as a specific instance where the principles and philosophies of planning should be applied."[37]

B.H. Kizer, chairman of the Washington State Planning Council, called on Silcox in Washington, D.C., on March 4. Silcox proposed to Kizer that some form of statutory control, such as a law requiring sustained yield cutting, be applied to the stands of timber to the west of the Mount Olympus National Monument so as to reassure proponents of a larger park that the timber involved would not be "ruthlessly slaughtered." Kizer informed him after returning to Washington State that the Planning Council's board members had reacted favorably to Silcox's proposal and would await a legal draft.[38] Though Silcox apparently did not follow up on this exchange, the Planning Council did recommend the idea to Buck.

Reticence in the Secretary of Agriculture's Office

In March of 1937, Irving Brant, editor of the *St. Louis Star Times* and a member of the New York-based Emergency Conservation Committee, wrote the secretary of agriculture in regard to the Olympic park controversy and furnished him with some data favoring the park. The letter was referred to the Forest Service to answer. That agency prepared a reply for Secretary Wallace's signature that questioned Brant's figures, presented some industry dependence effects, and advocated the sustained yield idea for public forests. The letter stated that the secretary backed wilderness reservations; however, trees are crops and "we can't tie it all up." The primitive area did the job and would not be violated. Secretary Wallace did not sign this letter; instead, James D. LeCron, his assistant, sent a copy of the proposed letter to Brant with an attached note saying it had been prepared by the Forest Service in answer to a memorandum from LeCron.[39]

Brant's six-page reply to the secretary challenged the dependency figures and the sustained yield data furnished by the Forest Service, and concluded that they were absurd. He also questioned the Forest Service's claim that it had voluntarily transferred lands to parks in the past, stating that he personally knew this was false. He said the Forest Service had "locked arm alliances" with industry against the inclusion of any merchantable timber within, for example, Sequoia National Park. Brant told the secretary that the Service's advice to him was bad and that he hoped the secretary would have nothing to do with their "vandalism."[40] Brant's position in the fourth estate as well as his general support of the Roosevelt administration yielded him much authority in the secretary's office.

The Forest Service also believed that Robert Marshall—a millionaire forester and a wilderness advocate, the director of forestry in the U.S. Bureau of Indian Affairs, the author of the recreation section of the "National Plan for American Forestry" and the founder of The Wilderness Society—had considerable influence over LeCron.[41] Chief Forester Silcox was personally fond of Marshall and had allowed him to express his views on wilderness at an earlier regional foresters' meeting in the winter of 1935. Although Marshall had received a cold reception from this group, he continued his efforts both through Secretary of the Interior Ickes personally and through Secretary of Agriculture Wallace's assistants.[42] Marshall created considerable discussion among the Washington office staff in late April, when he circulated an argument telling point-by-point why an area as large or larger than the proposed Mount Olympus park should be reserved from cutting. Marshall argued, as Heintzleman had earlier, that the Forest Service should ask for legislation keeping the Mount Olympus National Monument and Primitive Area free from logging but remaining under National Forest administration.[43] Assistant Regional Forester Brundage (on temporary duty in Washington, D.C., to prepare for possible new hearings) and Kneipp were asked to brief both pro and con arguments in Marshall's letter.[44]

Chief Silcox now defied convention: he brought Marshall into the Forest Service as chief of the Recreation and Lands Division in May 1937. Some observers thought that Marshall was creating so much agitation about national forest areas valuable for potential inclusion in the national park system that Silcox made a shrewd move by having him join the ranks where a measure of control could be exerted over his proposals.[45] Others thought that Marshall deliberately sought the transfer in order to influence the Forest Service to set aside more primitive areas.

Thus, there is some doubt about the effectiveness of Silcox's action, as Associate Chief Forester Clapp observed in a long memorandum to Kneipp on the Olympic park question and on the attitude in the secretary of agriculture's office. Clapp noted that when the Olympic matter was taken up the year before, the secretary had expressed doubts about the agency's position. When he finally concurred, the secretary had asked LeCron to make a special study of the situation. Clapp was not sure how fully LeCron had gone into the matter, though he knew LeCron had reviewed the evidence presented to the congressional committees and had been in touch with Brant and Bob Marshall, "the latter under the impression he was still in the Department of Interior." Clapp continued:

> In the brief and unsatisfactory discussion which I had with Le-Cron, he distinctly reflected the point of view of the . . . men listed above rather than that of the Forest Service. He advanced arguments such as those of Marshall. He raised questions in an offhand way which . . . would seem to attack the social and economic validity of attempts to use forest lands for the production of timber crops. He seemed to think that in the exchange of letters with Brant the Forest Service had all the worst of the argument. . . . As I have indicated to you he [LeCron] asked that Marshall be requested to put into memorandum form his point of view, etc., on the Park proposition. All of this taken together seems to me to make it necessary to review our statement in the light of LeCron's point of view, of Marshall's criticisms, etc., etc.

Clapp next listed several points for the staff to consider and check regarding LeCron's statements and Marshall's criticisms. In his conclusion, Clapp returned to the argument of the economic justification of stabilizing and maintaining communities and industries. He wondered if the Forest Service could disregard the sustained livelihood for even relatively small groups of people, such as "6,600 or 20,000." "After all, doesn't Marshall's form of question carried to its ultimate really mean that there is no economic justification for the use of land for timber production and that there is no economic justification for the National Forests?"[46]

The Washington office staff continued to rework their antipark arguments so as to make them acceptable to the secretary's office. In the process of doing this, Special Assistant Hammatt discovered that the potential dependency figures furnished by the regional office were about five times too large. He noted to Chief Silcox that "although the analysis shows that 78.8 persons per million feet annually are supported, this appears to be based on cordwood figures where 20 men per million feet cut are directly employed, whereas 4 per million are [employed] when pulp is secured through regular logging operations."[47]

Other drafts of material from Region Six argued that Forest Service administrative reservations (primitive areas) were sufficient to preserve representative stands of timber, and that "actual needs of the majority of people who may in the future visit this area should govern rather than the extremists on either side." One draft stated that there was little tendency for any large number of people to wander around for days. . . . It should be kept in mind that the entire country is now dependent on Washington and Oregon to meet the national needs for most of the supply of the various classes of timber products. . . . The Forest Service is committed to multiple use. . . . recreation can be had in non-virgin forests.[48]

With Congressman Wallgren pressing the Department of Agriculture for their report on the new park bill, the Forest Service's comments failed to satisfy the secretary's office. Kneipp noted to W.B. Greeley, former chief forester and now manager of the West Coast Lumbermen's Association, that it appeared Wallgren intended to push the matter. "The Committee might call up the Park bill on short notice," Kneipp wrote. "Any hearing is conjectural."[49]

Regional Forester Buck sought to delay any precipitate action on the park bill by suggesting a publicly announced six-year moratorium on timber cutting in the proposed park area. He told the chief forester that reason and calm might then prevail. Buck was informed that such a proposal was already on the secretary's desk to be signed and sent to the Public Lands Committee. The chief's office cautioned that until word came from the secretary, it was unwise to make any further moves toward a moratorium.[50]

Two days later Assistant Chief Forester Granger wrote a confidential letter to Buck advising him that LeCron and American Forestry Association officials William P. Wharton and Harris Reynolds would be arriving soon on an association trail riders trip into the Olympic Mountains. Granger confided that

> Clapp and I think you ought to know confidentially of the general attitude of the Secretary's Office on the Olympic Park bill. The Secretary himself is doubtful of the proper position of the Department, but is impressed with reserving larger areas of timber than the Forest Service proposes. He perhaps leans towards the park idea substantially. This is why he asked LeCron to study the matter on the ground. The psychology of Appleby [the other assistant to the secretary of agriculture besides LeCron who figured prominently in this case] and LeCron appears to be that the more timber reserved from cutting the better. . . . They seem to feel that communities dependent on timber can find some other way to meet their economic and social needs.
>
> This point of view has required us to rephrase our report to the House Committee, so as to considerably denature it—softpedal the economic side in order to have a show of getting it through the Department. Our letter to the Committee explain-

ing our report, for the Acting Secretary's signature, has required repeated revisions for Appleby. Clapp thinks LeCron has discussed the Park matter with Irving Brant. . . .

I do not need to point out the desirability of your contacting LeCron. . . . Obviously, it is desirable also to contact Wharton and Reynolds . . . [to] give assistance and information . . . and [to] indoctrinate them in any way that seems appropriate.[51]

Secretary Wallace did not sign the final revision (July 29, 1937) of the Forest Service's report on the current Wallgren bill until August 13, 1937. Even so, this much amended version, containing a six-page cover letter, sixteen sheets of supplementary material, and seven of tables, seemed to reiterate most of the Service's previous arguments about volumes of timber to be tied up and numbers of dependent families who would be left to shift for themselves.[52]

The Presidential Visit

A new factor appeared to create uncertainty for the Forest Service's anti-Olympic park campaign. Buck received word from E.A. Griffith, Works Progress Administration supervisor for Oregon, that the president and Mrs. Roosevelt planned to be in Oregon on September 29, visiting Bonneville Dam in the morning and Timberline Lodge on Mount Hood in the afternoon. They were to go to Seattle in the evening. Buck related to Associate Chief Clapp that "this may be a good opportunity to have the President say something about the National Forests. I will arrange with the W.P.A. for some sort of ceremonial at that time."[53]

Buck wrote to Silcox—who had been seriously ill a few weeks earlier but was recovering—regarding the presidential visit: "I hope you can be with this party. We should at least get out of it some recognition of the recreation values and work of the Forest Service. I shall also post people like the Governor and the Mayor of Portland to advise the President on National Forest recreation *vs.* the National Park set-up."[54]

It was then learned that the president was going to visit the Olympic Peninsula after going to Seattle. Elaborate preparations were begun: the Forest Service assigned personnel from all around the Pacific Northwest to help with the president's planned motor tour around the peninsula; numerous guides, drivers, and guards were needed for the excursion.

Buck set up headquarters in Port Angeles in the Lee Hotel pending the president's arrival by navy destroyer from Seattle. He later accompanied the presidential motorcade to Lake Crescent to spend the night. Buck telegraphed the Washington office on September 29: "President Roosevelt asked me to discuss with him opposition Olympic National Park tomorrow. Wire me any instructions." The Washington office wired back:

> Staff feels Olympic situation best discussed broadly rather than as specific conflict administrative programs. . . .
> Cite Olympic as specific example of rapidly growing number of cases where decision must be made as to whether large areas of federal lands and resources should be exclusively dedicated to single use . . . with total elimination of all industrial use of natural resources, or whether public interest best served by principles of land management under which spiritual and scenic values safeguarded . . . but social and economic needs of dependent communities also will be served by regulated use of other resources.[55]

Upon his arrival at Port Angeles, Roosevelt was impressed by a propark demonstration staged for his benefit. Buck was not effective in carrying out his telegraphed instructions, and, in fact, Roosevelt was antagonized by his arguments.[56]

The discussion in the president's Lake Crescent cabin was also attended by Olympic Forest Supervisor Bruckart, who noted some of Roosevelt's views on the park proposal. Comparing future public use of the Olympics with Yellowstone National Park, Roosevelt judged that the predicted large numbers of people who would visit the heavy timber stands in the future made it appear impossible and impractical to crowd them into the small area described in the current Wallgren bill. Bruckart reported that Roosevelt "stated that the area of the proposed park should be at least three times as large as the area in the present Wallgren Bill. . . . Congressman Smith pointed out that the industries in his district needed the timber to support the people in the district but the President indicated that the interest of the country as a whole could not be sacrificed to support local industry."[57]

This visit and the president's obvious support of a large park helped to break the Forest Service's efforts to control the situation. The agency had failed to convince others, too. District Ranger L.D. Blodgett, who three years before had been stationed at Port Angeles to counter the Park Service efforts in that city,[58] told Supervisor Bruckart: "I find more than ever that the public still does not know or does not believe that the Forest Service has done anything to protect national resources. In other words, the people of this town . . . sincerely believe that the Forest Service still allows unrestricted and destructive logging on the National Forests."[59]

The State Planning Council attempted to salvage some of the timber supply losses by composing a new park proposal that included a central park and scenic approach corridors managed by the Park Service. The forest away from the corridors would be managed by the Forest Service and the elk population by the Biological Survey.[60] Congressman Wallgren devised a counterproposal that legislated all of the Olympic National Forest into a recreation area supervised by the Park Service, with provisions for utilization of certain resources on certain areas under certain conditions.[61] The Forest Service liked neither of these proposals; but it did not find objectionable a proposition by W.B. Greeley, now representing the timber industry, for a recreation and protection area. The proposal provided a park with Forest Service-managed recreation areas around it, where timber could be utilized "under such methods as would preserve scenic and recreation values."[62]

Throughout October the Washington office apparently was not yet aware of what had occurred in the September presidential meeting with Buck at Lake Crescent. Kneipp commented to Silcox and other top staff on November 1 that "News clippings indicate that the President favors a Park considerably larger than that described in the pending Bill 4727. . . . As far as I am aware the President has not advised Secretary Wallace of what he thinks should be done."[63]

Silcox responded with a note to Kneipp on November 18, saying that he would "try to find out through the Secretary what the attitude of the President is toward extending the Park and try to arrange for a conference to determine what action should be taken." Neither Bruckart's account of the president's views nor a report on Buck's encounter seems to have reached the chief forester's office by that time. However, information about another elk hunt did arrive, described in some newspapers as a "drunken slaughter."[64]

The Washington staff, perhaps sensing that the battle was lost, were already looking for ways to avoid future political battles over parks. A confidential letter addressed to all regional foresters asked for suggestions on a proposal for an impartial committee to "consider rationally" all future national park proposals and any counterproposals made by the Forest Service. This idea was incorporated into a suggested letter from Wallace to the president, which argued that such a committee would "prevent controversy for all of us, and would be able to reach impartial conclusions more basically sound than any derived from present procedures." The letter concluded that the Department of Agriculture would abide by the committee's findings, "avoiding laying embarrassing matters on your desk."[65]

The Appleby Memorandum

The Olympic political struggle, however, was not yet over; the secretary of agriculture's office was yet to lay the "embarrassing matters" on the desk of the Forest Service rather than the reverse.

The Emergency Conservation Committee of New York had recently published a pamphlet called "Olympic Forests for a National Park." The author of this pamphlet, *St. Louis Star Times* editor Brant, again attacked the Forest Service and the lumber industry, challenging much of the data in previous Forest Service arguments. The pamphlet then discussed the recent elk "slaughter."[66]

Assistant Secretary of Agriculture Paul H. Appleby wrote a memorandum to Chief Silcox about the new pamphlet:

> As you know Irving Brant is a friend for whom we have much regard. The pamphlet he has written . . . we are not inclined at all to regard as the fanatical kind of thing often put out by that committee. It seems to me that this pamphlet puts the Forest Service in an embarrassing situation and really a situation that it earned for itself. I wonder if you don't agree with me. . . .
>
> I told Earle Clapp last summer that I felt the really smart and effective way for the Forest Service to meet this situation was for the Forest Service to propose to the Secretary establishment of a sanctuary in all the Olympic territory about which there has been discussion, and to propose to Congress legislation which would make the establishment of any sanctuary by any Secretary irrevocable except by Act of Congress.[67]

Wilderness enthusiast Robert Marshall's proposal for legislated primitive areas had reappeared.

Silcox discussed Appleby's memorandum with his staff, and it was decided to draft a bill providing legislative protection for an Olympic primitive area; this bill would offset the pending national park legislation. Assistant Chief Forester Granger noted that, with the exception of Associate Chief Clapp, it was generally agreed that the Forest Service had done all it could to present the arguments for economic use of the areas proposed for a park. Granger wrote: "Our position has not found much support in the Secretary's Office, has not the approval of the President, is not supported by the Senators from Washington, and

100

it seems idle for us to carry that campaign further. It is felt, however, that if an area is to be set up for the preservation of large timber, it should continue under Forest Service administration."[68]

Kneipp and Regional Forester Buck (in Washington, D.C., to prepare for hearings) drafted the Olympic forest wilderness bill in January 1938, telegraphing the Region Six office in Portland once or twice daily for a week to obtain detailed descriptions of the land for the proposal.

Buck then commented to Silcox on Appleby's memorandum, agreeing that the Forest Service was in an embarrassing situation, but describing Brant's pamphlet as a combination of truths, half-truths, and inaccuracies. He argued that

> between 33% and 50% of the population of Northwest Washington of one million people is dependent upon lumbering. Each one billion feet [of timber] withdrawn means a loss of support of upwards of 1,100 people. . . .
>
> . . . . Fifteen acres of . . . hemlock land will support a person permanently on a sustained yield basis. . . .
>
> It is agreed that a sanctuary of some kind should be recommended in the Olympics. Attached is a draft of a bill proposing the Olympic Forest Wilderness, which covers heavily timbered areas in addition to the present Wallgren Bill and serves to reserve an ample forest wilderness.
>
> As drawn the bill provides for no timber cutting, no highways, no reservoirs, for proper and effective game management, and for no development of large concessions for tourists but rather to retain a wilderness atmosphere in all developments.[69]

The text of the Olympic forest wilderness bill prohibited mining claims and the grazing of domestic livestock within the area covered. The bill also provided for purchase of nonfederal lands within the wilderness and authorized the necessary appropriations.[70]

Clapp supported the bill on the basis that it would keep the land under Forest Service jurisdiction and thwart the aggressive plans of the Interior Department. "If we concur," he noted, "in the proposal that the area must be made a national park because of timber stands of superlative quality, then we must also go along with other proposals for biological reservations. . . . If and when this area is absorbed, Interior will probably move on to another." Three members of the chief's staff opposed the Olympic forest wilderness bill, feeling that the Forest Service should not have its own national park and that if development was never to be permitted, the land did not belong in a national forest.[71]

Buck had sent a copy of the draft bill to the regional office in Portland. F.H. Brundage, as acting regional forester, discussed the measure with his staff division chiefs, and all concluded that they were against the bill. They believed the compromise proposal would raise serious doubts in the minds of the local citizens about the integrity of the Forest Service and that relations with the state as a whole would be seriously strained. Brundage observed in a confidential letter to Buck:

> Undoubtedly, the Region will be accused of bad faith by these people. . . . The limited funds available to the Region for these purposes [trails and recreation] . . . would be a serious drain. . . . We are inclined to question whether the retention of this area under Department of Agriculture administration would be advisable.

He then raised the question of integrity versus expediency:

> It is conceded that there is room for a difference of opinion on this matter and that from a national viewpoint the Chief or the Secretary may legitimately reverse the Region's previous position. We feel that such a reversal, however, would be an error in judgment in which much too great [a] weight would be given to the wilderness principle in the preservation of an area where the principal inspirational value would come from reading statistics drawn from cutting rather than personal experience on the ground. . . .
>
> . . . The Forest Service would be open to the accusation of reversing its position in a last ditch effort to retain jurisdiction of the area. . . . Loss of friends and prestige is certain to accrue in an attempt to gain doubtful benefits. The applause of the wilderness groups should be forthcoming but it will unquestionably be tempered by doubts of our sincerity.[72]

The President Calls the Shots

The Olympic forest wilderness bill never stimulated any public questioning of the integrity or the sincerity of the Forest Service. The agency had planned to have Representative Martin Smith introduce the bill and had submitted drafts to him for comment; however, the House calendar caused a problem before Smith could act.[73] Bruckhart informed the regional office that the *Abderdeen Daily World* of January 31 had published the story that the House Public Lands Committee has the call on the calendar this Wednesday and the proposed Olympic National Park is reported scheduled to be called up. Congressman Martin Smith secured an appointment with President Roosevelt at the White House at which the pending legislation was discussed. Smith said Roosevelt authorized him to see Senators Schwellenbach and Bone, and Representative Wallgren, Forest Service Chief Silcox, and Director of National Parks Cammerer and arrange for a conference with the entire group, himself, and the President in the near future.[74]

The meeting was indeed called, and Buck gave the following account of what happened in a letter from Washington to his Region Six office:

> The President directed that a line be agreed upon that would include all the Primitive Area to begin with, and other areas to make a large park. The conference to draw the line was held last Saturday, February 12, [and included] Congressmen Wallgren and Smith, Mr. Cammerer, Mr. Ben Thompson and one other Park Service man, Irving Brant, Mr. Silcox, and myself. The park proponents were given practically a free hand. . . .
>
> As soon as the Park Service has the description prepared, the bill will probably be amended to cover and presumably a favorable report will come from the Departments of Interior and Agriculture. The Forest Service it is understood will not protest this line. . . .
>
> Since the line was drawn in the presence of the Chief of the Forest Service and under the direction of the President, any protests will come solely from the economic interests, presumably, concerned.[75]

This letter signified the end of open and official resistance and opposition to the Olympic national park proposal by the U.S. Forest Service. As instructed by Buck, Brundage informed the staff of the Olympic National Forest that "by direction of the President a new proposed National Park boundary has been worked out by the Chief of the Park Service in cooperation with the Chief of the Forest Service. . . . The developments in Washington, D.C. make it imperative that the organization in Region Six take no partisanship in regard to the proposal. . . . Care should be taken to express no opinion on the merits of the proposal."[76]

Silcox finally replied to Appleby's memorandum. He pointed out that in his pamphlet Irving Brant had based his conclusions to a considerable degree on the printed report of the hearings on the Wallgren bill and on Kneipp's statements therein. The accuracy of the printed statements was open to question, he said, because the official reporter had later called on Kneipp, telling him there was much of his statement he did not get. Furthermore, Kneipp had not been given the expected opportunity to review or edit the transcript. Silcox then related what had happened with their sanctuary proposal and in the meeting with the president. He concluded, almost sadly, that "very little of the Olympic National Forest will be left under the jurisdiction of this Department if the boundaries proposed in the conference are ratified by Congress."[77]

Resistance to the larger park was continued by the lumber industry, Washington's Governor Martin, the State Planning Council, and various chambers of commerce throughout the spring, but an amended Wallgren bill (H.R. 10024) providing for a large park was passed by the House and the Senate on June 16, 1938.[78]

Summary

Reiteration of the Forest Service's values and premises became the major strategic response to the threat of the Wallgren bills. These values and premises were apparent in Kneipp's 1936 testimony before the House Committee on Public Lands, at the field level in a 1937 statement commenting on the second Wallgren bill, again in the draft letter prepared for the Public Lands Committee chairman, and, finally, in Regional Forester Buck's comments on the Appleby memorandum. The Forest Service was obviously sincere and very dedicated to its values; their staff fought hard, but found in the lack of support from the secretary of agriculture and the personal interventions of the president insurmountable odds. That there was no real economic scarcity of timber nationally and that none was foreseeable to nonforesters may also have contributed significantly to the defeat of the agency. Had the Service both anticipated the social and political forces at work and proposed Assistant Secretary Appleby's legislated sanctuary several years earlier (as they later successfully did in the Sawtooth park controversy in Idaho), they might have guided the forces of change and retained all of their domain. As it turned out, however, even if their last-minute effort had been completed, they probably still would have been too late.

Part 3　An Interpretation

6

Denouement: Insolvency and Foreclosure

This study was conducted to provide a case history of a long-standing bureaucratic rivalry; it also meant to test a set of theoretical assumptions as to the influence of value orientation upon the capacity of an organization to respond to changed expectations of powerful interests in its operating environment. The study is significant in the case of the national forests as an example of the many conflicts between two rival agencies over land use policy affecting the public domain. Philosophically, this rivalry is representative of the long history of clashes between progressive utilitarianism and the romantic movement.

The history of these conflicts from 1904 on suggests that the National Park Service and a number of national parks might never have been created had Chief Forester Gifford Pinchot and his followers in the Forest Service permitted accommodation of at least some of the demands of aesthetic recreation groups.[1] However, commitment to certain values and premises led them to initially oppose those groups, and conflicts have henceforth repeatedly occurred, right down to the Alaska National Interest Lands Act of 1980. A brief respite, while the Forest Service was still recovering from the dismissal of Chief Pinchot, ended when the National Park Service was created through the efforts of aesthetic recreationists in 1916. Since then the conflict has taken on a more competitive quality, with the Forest Service clinging to its original values while also working to enhance its recreation image sufficiently to avoid losing ground to the rival Park Service.

The Alternative Hypotheses

Two alternative hypotheses were considered in the theoretical analysis for the study. The first, suggested by the work of political scientist Grant McConnell, was that the crop production orientation of the Forest Service was a result of the agency's pragmatic accommodation of the local power sources making up its social environment. In addition, McConnell argued that rather than regulating the sector of business it was intended to control, the agency followed only the criterion of "the greatest good of the greatest number" as a moral guide. McConnell felt this was exceedingly subjective and vague; therefore, it was only natural that they would wander before "the pressures of all the winds that blew" and dispose of the resources according to their power needs.[2] If this was so, the rational pursuit of power would dictate accommodation of all strong political power, even if it came from preservationist and recreational groups.

Herbert Kaufman's *The Forest Ranger,* a study of the Forest Service describing the intense occupational socialization of its members, reinforced the author's personal observations of the agency and led to the development and, ultimately, the adoption of the alternative hypothesis assuming value orientation and a tendency toward system closure. That hypothesis, based also on work by political scientist Ashley Schiff,[3] suggested that a perpetuated value orientation has tended to close off the Forest Service system from innovative response to change, resulting in the loss of political "turf." Thus, instead of rationally pursuing all new power sources as an open system would, the agency appeared to ignore or misperceive them.

Defined as conceptions of the desirable which influence action, values were pointed out to be one of the two components of value orientation. Existential premises, the other component, are assumptions about the nature of the world or are what one assumes to be cognitive facts. These two components serve as a shared frame of reference for decision making by a particular group or organization.

Two core theories were assumed in this study of the Forest Service's decision-making processes. The first, sustained yield theory, is composed of the existential premises of stability, land scarcity, and certainty, and the value that a *closed economy* should prevail; the second, utilitarian theory, combines the premise of timber primacy and the values of telic forestry, scientific elitism, and technocracy.

Decision making was described as determined by an organization's structure, by the information available to the members, and by shared motivations, including value orientation. Information tends to be perceived selectively by members, and the organization's structure of roles and internal and external relations further determines that body's activities in response to stimuli.

Not only the Forest Service's value orientation but also its organizational structure were important to the agency's decision-making process. The partially closed structure of the Service not only ensured the rigid perpetuation of certain values, but it also discouraged innovation in response to outside change. Similarly, Fremont Lyden has shown how the values and the highly integrated structure of the U.S. Bureau of Reclamation tended to close that system's perception of change, resulting in a weakening of a once strong organization.[4]

The structure of the Forest Service caused rigidity because it was patterned after the eighteenth-century European, bureaucratic "machine" model, which emphasized reliability of behavior to maintain central control. Use of this model tends to result in increased impersonality and increased internalization of rules and values, to the point where means become substituted for ends. Such structural characteristics can be expected to prevent anticipation of change and responsiveness to new sources of power in the organization's environment. Thus, an innovative response to a new stimulus would not be predicted. On the contrary, the opposite would tend to occur. That is, a consolidative response—an attempt to satisfy external forces for change by reordering or revising programs within the organization's existing framework of values and norms—would be expected. A problem with consolidative behavior, however, is that by the time an adequate response is made, the organization tends to be on the defensive and its options are limited. Thus, the organization has less control over its future and its domain than has an organization which anticipates institutional trends and adapts innovatively to change.

Assuming that the Forest Service's value orientation would be perpetuated by the structural characteristics of that organization, I had hypothesized that examination of any major conflict in which the Service became involved would disclose a reiteration of its value orientation, in whole or in part, in support of the agency's responses. Thus, when confronted with changes affecting the welfare of the organization and requiring innovative or nonprogrammed decision making, the Forest Service would first try to control its environment by reemphasizing traditional programs and values; second, when faced with defeat, it would act consolidatively by developing a new program that fit within the framework of existing organizational norms and values. Analysis of the case essentially sustained the hypothesis.

Establishment in 1909 of the Mount Olympus National Monument on national forest lands was accomplished, despite Forest Service objections, to protect the Olympic elk. Throughout its history, the Forest Service continued to perceive that land and its forests primarily as a wood supply source to meet an impending scarcity of timber. In the early period, the political forces concerned with the elk problem and the area's recreation potential were relatively uncohesive and, even though national park bills were introduced in Congress, no serious threat was felt.

This situation changed in 1933, however, with the coincident public arousal over the elk problem, the election of a new propark president, and the transfer of the jurisdiction of Mount Olympus National Monument to the Park Service via executive order. The domain of the Forest Service was now severely threatened.

The personal intervention of President Franklin D. Roosevelt generated two major consolidative responses on the part of the Forest Service: the first was the 1936 administrative enlargement of the adjacent Olympic Primitive Area after the president had suggested inclusion of more forest land within the national monument; the second was the last-minute drafting by the Forest Service of the Olympic forest wilderness bill following the 1937 presidential visit to the Olympics, in which Roosevelt advocated a large national park. This belated effort was opposed by some members of the Forest Service's Washington office staff and by majorities of the regional and forest level staffs. The issue was decided a few days later when the president called the agency heads and the Washington State congressional delegation to his office, directing that a large park be agreed upon, with boundary lines drawn to include much of the timbered area the Forest Service wished to retain. This would not have been possible, of course, if the president had not recognized strong political support for his position.

In its arguments to various interest groups, to the Park Service, to the secretary of agriculture and his assistants, before the House Public Lands Committee, and to the president himself, the Forest Service continually referenced directly or implicitly to at least some of the values and premises hypothesized for the study of this case. Indeed, reference to these elements generally constituted the agency's major defense of its position. It is obvious throughout the case that Forest Service personnel were quite committed to, were sincere about, and honestly believed in the validity of their definition of the situation. The Service made a great effort to ensure that its conception prevailed and, when they failed, the field staff argued that it would be better to lose than to compromise their integrity.

As noted earlier, other factors contributing to the defeat of the Forest Service in the battle for the Olympics were the withdrawal of active support by the secretary of agriculture, the personal intervention of President Roosevelt, and the existence of, in the midst of the Great Depression, no real economic scarcity of timber nationally.

110

The Policy—Bureaucratic Context

This case had certain impacts on the development of natural resource policy for the United States government, and it reveals some key differences in how agencies fight for bureaucratic turf.

President Franklin D. Roosevelt's strong commitment to preservation as a legitimate alternative to utilitarian use of natural resources left a lasting mark on national policy and the concept of multiple use. This commitment was also evidenced in Secretary of the Interior Ickes's efforts to integrate all natural resource agencies under a single department of conservation.

The effect of a strong secretary on the Department of the Interior revived that department and fueled its long-standing feud with the Department of Agriculture, resulting in an aggressive political campaign by both the Interior Department and its agency, the Park Service.

The words "multiple use" did not appear in Forest Service rationale until the late 1930s and the concept was not prescribed by its manual until 1958. Indeed, the Service's adherence to utilitarian values had long been considered quite compatible with the crop production ideology of the Agriculture Department. The change to the multiple use concept, listing outdoor recreation first among the uses of national forests, seems to have been stimulated by Park Service competition. As Richard Polenberg has observed, however, before the 1960 Multiple Use Act, Pinchot's followers seldom deviated from his pronouncement that "a forest is a crop, and forestry is uniformly classed as a branch of agriculture."[5]

Interestingly, a slight difference was evident in the interpretations of the Forest Service's value orientation by the national officers and the field personnel. Officers in the nation's capital saw sustained yield and the utilitarian theory as something to be accomplished within the national jurisdiction; field workers, however, considered this orientation as applicable on a discrete basis to each self-contained planning unit or working circle. This latter approach tended to limit the possibility of employing multiple use criteria.

The antipolitical attitude of the Forest Service was clearly evidenced at the congressional hearings, where both the secretary of the interior and the Park Service director testified, while neither the secretary of agriculture nor the chief forester did. Furthermore, the Park Service was active in bargaining with the public at all levels; the Forest Service was not, perhaps because of its traditional distrust of the political system. Historically, the foresters seem to have preferred remaining aloof from any system that might have been construed as seeking control of the land for its exploitation. In keeping with the Service's policy of minimizing political involvement while following a "rational economic" basis of action, legislative bodies have been viewed by foresters as agents of special interests. Consequently, as Maass points out, among the foresters confidence has rested primarily in technical rationality, with the executive branch technicians seen as those best qualified to define the common good in the subject at hand.[6]

The emphasis on technical rationality, on the production of tangible goods and services, and on the justification of this through ideology or a highly enculturated value orientation should lead to patterned behavior. Further examination of Forest Service administrative behavior should reveal comparable cases.

The Comparative Context

It should come as no surprise that the Forest Service struggle over the Olympic National Forest is anything but unique. In a long series of similar controversies, the most prolonged was the thirty-four-year Park Service campaign begun in 1916 to acquire the Grand Tetons and the Jackson Hole area in Wyoming. There, the Forest Service fought to defend both timber cutting and local grazing ranges for sheep and cattle against the spectacular wilderness appeal of the nation's most rugged range of mountains. However, the lack of park support at both local and state levels made Forest Service opposition doubly hard for the Park Service to overcome, and though this agency had the influential backing of the president, the Rockefellers, and other powerful conservation groups, the Forest Service doggedly held on. A bill transferring the Grand Teton Mountains to the Park Service was finally passed in Congress on February 26, 1929, but the fight over the Jackson Hole area below the mountains was to continue through the 1930s. Assistant Regional Forester C.J. Olsen of Ogden wrote in 1936 that, while the Forest Service had successfully blocked the proposed Sawtooth National Park in Idaho, "we are not quite as fortunate in the Grand Teton National Park case but believe we will get that settled before long, approximately satisfactorily. Satisfactorily, of course, would be that the Park Service [would] get none of the area." Despite Forest Service and local resistance, on March 15, 1943, President Roosevelt proclaimed the Jackson Hole National Monument, transferring both donated private land and 100,000 acres more of the Teton National Forest to the Park Service.[7]

Another protracted controversy was that leading to the establishment of Kings Canyon National Park in California. In that granite-walled scenic region, the utilitarian values defended by the Forest Service were primarily related to "water storage for irrigation and hydroelectric power development, timber which will eventually have economic significance, forage values and other economic possibilities." Backed by the Sierra Club and other strong conservation groups, Congress transferred Kings Canyon from the Forest to the Park Service in 1940.[8]

More recently the Forest Service lost control over the North Cascades National Park in Washington State. Arising as a wilderness controversy in the 1930s, the issue was revived by the Sierra Club and other groups in the 1950s. The campaign developed, and President John F. Kennedy entered the fray by ordering a joint Forest Service-Park Service study and report on the area. As with the Olympics, a broad base of both local and national support developed for a North Cascades national park. The Forest Service opposed the park, expounding all its traditional values in defense. Clearcut logging was extended up the valleys of the Suiattle and White Chuck rivers and upon the flanks of Mount Baker, as far and as rapidly as possible in order to keep these areas out of the proposed park. Again, a legislated wilderness area was proposed, to exist under Forest Service jurisdiction. However, the combination of the clearcutting extensions and a critical television documentary film polarized public opinion against the Forest Service. A bill providing for a large park and two additional legislated wilderness areas was signed by President Lyndon Johnson in 1968.[9]

The Park Service was created in 1916, and controversies involving the Park Service-Forest Service rivalry have continued since then. Of eleven proposed land transfers objected to by Chief Forester R.Y. Stuart in his 1932 letter to Park Director Horace Albright, seven were ultimately shifted to the Park Service. Among these seven were the Redwood Canyon and Mineral King additions to Sequoia National Park, the Wawona addition to Yosemite National Park, and a portion of the proposed Cedar Breaks area in Utah. The Park Service recommended more transfers of Forest Service lands in its report on land planning to the National Resources Planning Board in November 1934, and so the conflicts persisted.[10]

The Theoretical Context

This case study has suggested that the Forest Service failed to innovate in response to social change partly because of their organizational structure, which closed its system to the perception of change. This situation prevailed in the hierarchy up to the top Washington, D.C., levels.

To explain why system closure extended even to the highest levels of the Forest Service, it is useful to look at one of the structural models of social system organization postulated by Talcott Parsons. Parsons suggests that formal organizational systems exhibit three hierarchical levels of responsibility and control: a technical, a managerial, and an institutional level.[11]

At the lowest, or technical, level the effective application of a technology functions to produce some product or service. The operating requirements guiding the efforts of the technical level of the organization are primarily those relating to the particular technical function. Long-range planning of successive crops of timber takes place at this level. The logical model for accomplishing complete technical rationality of such a sustained yield is a closed system.[12] Sustained production of timber can be planned by eliminating uncertainty, closing the planning system by including only predefined variables associated with achieving organizational goals, and subjecting the variables to a mechanistic control network.

According to Parsons, the managerial level services the technical level of the organization, mediating between that plane and the clientele who directly use its output. In addition, the managerial level obtains the technical resources necessary for organizational functioning; it controls the technical level by deciding on the regular tasks to be carried out and by establishing operating and "housekeeping" policies. The constant updating of the agency operations manual would exemplify this level.

At the top of this organizational model is the institutional level. Parsons points out that, being a part of the broader social system or society, any organization presumably has some purpose to accomplish for the larger society, as well as a means of relating to it. The organization is thus able to obtain authority and monetary resources from that larger entity as a result of the social acceptance of the organization's services or products. The institutional level relates and explains the organization to the rest of society, so as to maintain its legitimacy and to obtain the support needed to implement its programs. Essentially dealing with uncertainty, this level of the organization continuously attempts to adapt the organization to changes in society so as to keep the necessary social support.

Each of the levels requires a qualitatively different operating perspective for effective functioning, according to Parsons. In the case of the Forest Service, however, it was found that attributes of the technical level of the agency, particularly the premise of future certainty (see p. 22), extended all the way up through the organization's hierarchy. In a sense, the technical sustained yield theory (the applied core theory of forestry used by the technical level; see p. 22) had become reified.[13] Production techniques, consumption patterns, and values were assumed to be static. The means had become the goal.

This goal substitution process often occurs when the mandate of an organization fails to describe its intended purpose adequately or precisely enough to allow measurement of achievement. Such ambiguity of purpose tends to emphasize a technology without evaluating its external, societal impact. As Professor George Shipman has stated, in this type of situation where the means become the ends, "the real objective of the organization becomes system maintenance; the motivating values reflect vested interests in the continuation of organizational existence."[14]

When the attributes of the technical core—particularly certainty—are found throughout the hierarchy of an organization, the absence of a definable institutional level is indicated. The lack of this level is further indicated in this particular case by the nonexistence of a sharp distinction between managerial and institutional matters. At the institutional level we rarely observed the broad social assessments normally made to relate the organization's efforts to the rest of society. More often noted were the instrumental rationales of the technology. This situation suggests a relatively closed system, particularly since there were continuous attempts to exclude or neutralize all outside influences that did not agree with the technical assessments.

An organization imbued with certainty suggests not only a high level of integration and a rigid perpetuation of value orientation, but also a task environment that does not sufficiently challenge the assumptions on which the organization bases its actions. In the early years of this case, the Forest Service's insulation from political pressure in the Department of Agriculture, its shield of professionalism, its diversionary use of primitive areas, and its development of political power through the use of "key men" from certain clientele groups kept the recreation interests from wielding enough power to challenge the assumptions on which the Forest Service acted.[15] Thus, precedent in the form of value orientation, rather than innovation, guided the Service's decisions.

James D. Thompson has observed, however, that ultimately task environment elements do achieve the power to challenge an organization's assumptions, even though such power may only be exercised in the case of bankruptcy, monetary or otherwise." Bankruptcy, or "insolvency" in this sense, relates to the "political marketplace." As money is the medium of exchange in the economy, power acts as the same in the polity. The survival and growth of government institutions depend on their capacity to generate inputs of support, both at the grass roots and the national levels. An agency needs to develop excess capital, a surplus of power supports, in order to be able to defend itself against political threats. A lack of sufficient power supports is a condition of "insolvency" under these circumstances. When a competing bureau that has an apparent surplus of power appears on the scene, its displacement of the less "solvent" bureau is to be expected.[16]

In the Olympic National Park controversy, the Forest Service's tenacious commitment to its value orientation prevented it from meeting new demands. The agency's goal—to commit virtually all of the timber of the Olympic National Forest to satisfy the demands of limited power groups—left it without the resources to obtain the support or neutrality of other interested groups. The power of those groups, therefore, flowed to the competing bureau.

The strength of those other interested groups was only slowly perceived; the legitimacy of their demands was denied to the very end. Eventual moves by the Forest Service to meet the new demands came too late to retain political support. Critical elements of national leadership became convinced that the Forest Service's administration was impoverished. Foreclosure ensued . . . and Congress placed the resources under the competing organization's control.

Notes

Correspondence is cited in the Notes as follows: those from the Seattle Federal Records Center are by Forest Service file designation, box number, and "SEA"; those from the chief's office in Washington, D.C., are by Forest Service file designation, then "WASO." Material from the minutes of the Forest Service Executive Committee can be found in the National Archives, Record Group 95, Washington, D.C.

A sample entry might read thus: "LP Bdrys., Olympic, Box 3517, SEA." This means that the memorandum was classified under land planning and boundaries, for the Olympic National Forest, and was located in that folder, in box number 3517, in the Seattle Federal Records Center. Olympic is sometimes shortened to "Oly." "S" and "L" are other Forest Service filing designations, standing for timber sales and lands.

Preface

1. Talcott Parsons, "General Theory in Sociology," in *Sociology Today*, ed. R.K. Merton, Leonard Broom, and L.S. Cottrell, Jr., 2 vols. (New York: Basic Books, 1959), 1:10-16.

2. Max Weber, "Bureaucracy," in *From Max Weber: Essays in Sociology*, ed. Hans Gerth and C. Wright Mills (New York: Oxford Univ. Press, 1946), p. 199.

3. Kenneth McNeil, "Understanding Organizational Power: Building on the Weberian Legacy," *Administrative Science Quarterly* 23 (Mar. 1978): 65-90.

Chapter 1

1. Roderick Nash, *Wilderness and the American Mind* (New Haven: Yale Univ. Press, 1967), pp. 44-45; James P. Gilligan, "The Development of Policy

and Administration of Forest Service Primitive and Wilderness Areas in the Western United States" (Ph.D. diss., Univ. of Michigan, 1953), p. 8.

2. Russell Lynes, *The Tastemakers* (New York: Grosset & Dunlop, 1954), pp. 30-35; Nash, *Wilderness,* pp. 78-83, 159.

3. Hans Huth, *Nature and the American: Three Centuries of Changing Attitudes* (Berkeley: Univ. of California Press, 1957), p. 166; Nash, *Wilderness,* p. 141.

4. George Perkins Marsh, *Man and Nature* (London: Charles Scribner, 1864), passim.

5. Samuel T. Dana and Sally Fairfax, *Forest and Range Policy,* 2d ed. (New York: McGraw-Hill, 1979), p. 42.

6. Ibid., p. 42.

7. Gifford Pinchot, *The Fight for Conservation* (1910; reprint ed., Seattle: Univ. of Washington Press, 1967), p. 16; Harold K. Steen's *The U.S. Forest Service: A History* (Seattle: Univ. of Washington Press, 1976) provides (in chapter 2, pp. 26-37) the definitive statement of this legislative history.

8. Henry Gannett, "The Forests of the United States," in *19th Annual Report of the U.S. Geological Survey, 1897-1898,* part 5 (Washington: U.S. Govt. Printing Office, 1899), p. 2; Norman Wengert, "Changing Relations Between Government and the Forest Products Industries: An Exploration of Policy Processes," in *Proceedings of the First National Colloquium on the History of the Forest Products Industry* (New Haven: Forest History Society, 1967), p. 34.

9. Nash, *Wilderness,* pp. 120, 132. See also Samuel P. Hays, *Conservation and the Gospel of Efficiency* (New York: Atheneum, 1969), p. 191. Lawrence Rakestraw, *A History of Forest Conservation in the Pacific Northwest, 1891-1915* (New York: Arno Press, 1979), pp. 29-30; Gilligan, "The Development of Policy," p. 37.

10. Gilligan, "The Development of Policy," pp. 48-49.

11. Nash, *Wilderness,* pp. 149-50, 150-53; Theodore Roosevelt, "Forests and Foresters," in *Theodore Roosevelt's America,* ed. Farida Wiley (Garden City: Anchor Books, 1962), p. 295; Hays, *Conservation,* p. 189.

12. Hays, *Conservation,* pp. 196, 197-98; Theodore Roosevelt, "Forestry and Irrigation," in Wiley, *Theodore Roosevelt's America,* pp. 296-97; Gifford Pinchot, "Government Forestry Abroad," *Publications of the American Economic Association* 6, no. 3 (1891): 30; Gilligan, "The Development of Policy," p. 52. See also H. Louise Peffer, *The Closing of the Public Domain* (Palo Alto: Stanford Univ. Press, 1951), p. 175; and Henry Clepper, "The Forest Service Backlashed," *Forest History* 11 (Jan. 1968): 9. Bernhard E. Fernow, *Economics of Forestry* (New York: Thomas Y. Crowell, 1902), pp. 85-87.

13. Andrew Denny Rodgers, III, *Bernhard Eduard Fernow: A Story of North American Forestry* (Princeton: Princeton Univ. Press, 1951), pp. 277-303; Hays, *Conservation,* pp. 195-96; Stephen Fox, *John Muir and His Legacy: The American Conservation Movement* (Boston: Little, Brown, 1981), p. 130; Nash, *Wilderness,* p. 139.

14. Harold T. Pinkett, *Gifford Pinchot: Private and Public Forester* (Ur-

bana: Univ. of Illinois Press, 1970), p. 53; Martin L. Fausold, *Gifford Pinchot, Bull Moose Progressive* (Palo Alto: Stanford Univ. Press, 1961), p. 21.

15. Nash, *Wilderness,* pp. 161, 164; Lewis A. Coser, *The Functions of Social Conflict* (New York: Free Press, 1956), p. 92; Hays, *Conservation,* p. 196; Donald C. Swain, "The Passage of the National Park Service Act of 1916," *Wisconsin Magazine of History* 50, no. 1 (1966): 5.

16. Gilligan, "The Development of Policy," p. 62.

17. Ibid., p. 64. See also Clepper, "The Forest Service Backlashed," p. 9. Swain, "The Passage of the National Park Service Act," p. 5.

18. Henry S. Graves to district forester, San Francisco, Feb. 7, 1913, in L, District Policy, Boundaries, Box 12372, SEA.

19. Nash, *Wilderness,* p. 170.

20. Ibid., pp. 180-81; Swain, "The Passage of the National Park Service Act," p. 5.

21. Gilligan, "The Development of Policy," pp. 71-72.

22. Ibid., p. 74; Donald N. Baldwin, "An Historical Study of the Western Origin, Application, and Development of the Wilderness Concept, 1919-1933" (Ph.D. diss., Univ. of Denver, 1965), p. 17. This work has since been published in part as *The Quiet Revolution: Grass Roots of Today's Wilderness Preservation Movement* (Boulder, Colo.: Pruett, 1972).

23. Gilligan, "The Development of Policy," p. 92; Baldwin, "An Historical Study," pp. 86, 334.

24. Donald C. Swain, *Federal Conservation Policy, 1921-1933,* Univ. of California Publications in History, no. 76 (Berkeley, 1963), pp. 135, 202; Gilligan, "The Development of Policy," p. 93.

25. U.S., Congress, Senate Document 117, 69th Cong., 1st sess., 1926, p. 42.

26. Baldwin, "An Historical Study," p. 257; Gilligan, "The Development of Policy," p. 130.

27. Gilligan, "The Development of Policy," pp. 97, 124.

28. Ibid., pp. 101-8.

29. Ibid., pp. 107, 127; Baldwin, "An Historical Study," pp. 272-73; Gilligan, "The Development of Policy," p. 129.

30. Gilligan, "The Development of Policy," p. 128.

31. Ibid., pp. 120-24.

32. Chief Forester R.Y. Stuart to National Park Service Director H.M. Albright, Oct. 11, 1930; quoted in U.S., Congress, House, Committee on Public Lands, *Hearings on the Proposed Mount Olympus National Park,* 74th Cong., 2d sess., 1936, p. 235.

33. Albright to Stuart, June 16, 1931, copy in L Boundaries, Umpqua, Diamond Lake, Box 40073, SEA; Stuart to Albright, Mar. 3, 1932, copy in LP Boundaries, Rogue River, Box 40073, SEA.

34. Record Group 95, "Minutes of the Service Committee," Aug. 18, 1932.

35. Gilligan, "The Development of Policy," p. 148; Harold L. Ickes, *The Secret Diary of Harold L. Ickes,* 3 vols. (New York: Simon & Schuster, 1954), 2: 584.

Chapter 2

1. Grant McConnell, *Private Power and American Democracy* (New York: Vintage Books, 1970), pp. 360-61.

2. Ibid., p. 200.

3. Ashley L. Schiff, "Innovation and Administrative Decision-Making: The Conservation of Land Resources," *Administrative Science Quarterly* 11, no. 1 (1966): 3, 5; Parsons, "General Theory in Sociology," 1: 17-23; Schiff, "Innovation and Administrative Decision-Making," p. 3.

4. Schiff, "Innovation and Administrative Decision-Making," p. 5.

5. See Rollo Handy, *The Measurement of Values* (St. Louis: Warren H. Green, 1970), pp. 214-15, for support for this approach. I am also aware of other approaches to value analysis, such as that of Milton Rokeach, *The Nature of Human Values* (New York: Free Press, 1973), but at present I agree with Handy's assessment of Rokeach's work.

6. Wilbert E. Moore, "Occupational Socialization," in *Handbook of Socialization Theory and Research,* ed. David Goslin (Chicago: Rand McNally, 1973), pp. 879-80.

7. Benjamin Schneider, Douglas T. Hall, and Harold T. Nygren, "Self Image and Job Characteristics as Correlates of Changing Organizational Identification," *Human Relations* 24 (Oct. 1971): 397.

8. Jerome S. Bruner, *On Knowing: Essays for the Left Hand* (Cambridge: Harvard Univ. Press, 1964), p. 141.

9. Moore, "Occupational Socialization," pp. 876-77.

10. Victor Thompson, *Bureaucracy and Innovation* (University, Ala.: Univ. of Alabama Press, 1969), p. 95.

11. Daniel Katz and Robert L. Kahn, *The Social Psychology of Organizations,* 2d ed. (New York: John Wiley, 1978), p. 388.

12. Louis C. Gawthrop, *Bureaucratic Behavior in the Executive Branch* (New York: Free Press, 1969), pp. 134-40.

13. Ibid., p. 140.

14. Frederick Mosher, *Democracy and the Public Service* (New York: Oxford Univ. Press, 1968), p. 152; Howard Aldrich and Jeffrey Pfeffer, "Environments of Organizations," *Annual Review of Sociology* 2 (1976): 98.

15. David Segal and Daniel Willick, "The Reinforcement of Traditional Career Patterns in Agencies Under Stress," *Public Administration Review* 29 (Jan.-Feb. 1968): 30. See also Harold Seidman, *Politics, Position and Power* (New York: Oxford Univ. Press, 1970), pp. 111-16. Coser, *The Functions of Social Conflict,* p. 103.

16. Mosher, *Democracy and the Public Service,* p. 152; Aldrich and Pfeffer, "Environments of Organizations," p. 97.

17. Herbert Kaufman, *The Forest Ranger* (Baltimore: Johns Hopkins Press, 1960), passim.

18. Ibid., pp. 234-35.

19. Gifford Pinchot, *The Use Book: Regulations and Instructions for the Use of the National Forest Reserves* (Washington: U.S. Govt. Printing Office,

1906), p. 150; Hans Rosenberg, *Bureaucracy, Aristocracy, and Autocracy, The Prussian Experience, 1660-1815* (Boston: Beacon Press, 1966), p. 181; Pinchot, "Government Forestry Abroad," p. 18; Brandis to Pinchot, Feb. 14-18, 1897, Gifford Pinchot Papers, Box 968, Series 8, Library of Congress, Washington, D.C.; Von Herbert Hesmer, *Leben und Werk Von Dietrich Brandis* (Westdeutcher: Verlag, 1975), pp. 370-71. The history of bureaucratic promotion from within as a Prussian absolutist device and many of the other practices to ensure bureaucratic conformity observed by Kaufman in *The Forest Ranger* can be traced in Rosenberg's *Bureaucracy, Aristocracy, and Autocracy*.

20. David Cushman Coyle, *Conservation, An American Story of Conflict and Accomplishment* (New Brunswick: Rutgers Univ. Press, 1957), p. 40.

21. M. Nelson McGeary, *Gifford Pinchot: Forester-Politician* (Princeton: Princeton Univ. Press, 1960), p. 34; Rodgers, *Bernhard Eduard Fernow*, pp. 218-19; Coyle, *Conservation, An American Story*, p. 54; Rodgers, *Bernhard Eduard Fernow*, p. 15; McGeary, *Gifford Pinchot*, p. 30; Rakestraw, *A History of Forest Conservation in the Pacific Northwest*, p. 326.

22. Donald F. Cate, "Recreation and the U.S. Forest Service" (Ph.D. diss., Stanford Univ., 1963), p. 376.

23. Kaufman, *The Forest Ranger*, p. 197. Some years after the data for this study were collected, Kaufman concluded from subsequent research that many organizations cannot change because of what he calls "templates," which are the result of "training, conditioning, learning, socialization, acculturation, or brainwashing" [H. Kaufman, "The Natural History of Human Organizations," *Administration and Society* 7, no. 2 (Aug. 1975): 131-49]. His conclusion seems to support the value orientation hypothesis of this study.

24. James March and Herbert Simon, *Organizations* (New York: John Wiley, 1958), pp. 150-51.

25. Robert K. Merton, *The Sociology of Science* (Chicago: Univ. of Chicago Press, 1973), p. 262.

26. See John Stuart Mill, "Nature," in *Readings in Philosophy*, ed. John H. Randall, Jr., and E.U. Shirk (New York: Barnes and Noble, 1950), pp. 44-70. See also WJ McGee, "Scientific Work of the Department of Agriculture," *Popular Science Monthly* 76 (June 1910): 524. To McGee technology and science were the government's tools for social reform akin to that seen by Mill and positivistic sociologists from Saint Simon and Comte to Lester Ward. See Lester Ward, *Dynamic Sociology*, 2 vols. (1883; reprint ed., New York: Greenwood Press, 1968), 2: 111-57, 231-49. See also the discussion of utilitarian positivistic sociology versus romanticism in Alvin Gouldner, *The Coming Crisis of Western Sociology* (New York: Avon, 1971), pp. 88-107.

WJ McGee credits Hamilton, as well as Lester Ward, for his philosophic views. Mill and Hamilton were much in agreement, although Mill criticized Hamilton in his biography. Ward supported "scientific utilitarianism"—technocratic governmental action, with social and natural forces being purposefully directed toward a rational organization of happiness for all [*Dynamic Sociology* (New York: Greenwood Press, 1968), 2: 155-56].

27. Ernest M. Gould, "Forestry and Recreation," *Harvard Forest Papers* 6

(1962): 3; Adam Schwappach, *Forestry*, trans. Fraser Story and Eric Nobbs (London: J.M. Dent, 1904), p. 6; Ernest M. Gould, "The Future of Forests in Society," *Forestry Chronicle* 40, no. 4 (1964): 432-33.

28. Gould, "Forestry and Recreation," p. 3.

29. Gouldner, *The Coming Crisis*, p. 66.

30. John D. Bennett, "Economics and the Folklore of Forestry" (Ph.D. diss., Syracuse Univ., 1968), pp. 9-15.

31. McGee, "Scientific Work of the Department of Agriculture," p. 529; Thomas R. Waggener, *Some Economic Implications of Sustained Yield as a Forest Regulation Model*, Institute of Forest Products, Univ. of Washington, Contemporary Forest Paper no. 6 (Seattle, 1969), pp. 13-21.

32. Arthur Maass, "Conservation, Political and Social Aspects," *International Encyclopedia of the Social Sciences*, 18 vols. (New York: Free Press, 1968), 3: 272-73. Compare this with the positivist, utopian socialist view of Henri Saint Simon's and August Comte's followers, who saw scientists as a new elite, providing a new social map for society (Gouldner, *The Coming Crisis*, pp. 99-100), and Lester Ward's view that government could be run by social scientists, who would "render harmless those forces now seen to be working evil results, and to render useful those now running to waste" (*Dynamic Sociology*, 2: 249).

33. Hays, *Conservation*, p. 271; Reinhard Bendix, *Max Weber: An Intellectual Portrait* (Garden City: Anchor, 1962), pp. 425-30; Michael J. Lacey, "The Mysteries of Earthmaking Dissolve: A Study of Washington's Intellectual Community and the Origins of American Environmentalism in the Late Nineteenth Century" (Ph.D. diss., George Washington Univ., 1979), pp. 105-30, passim.

34. Whitney R. Cross, "WJ McGee and the Idea of Conservation," *The Historian* 15 (Spring 1953): 156; McGee, "Scientific Work of the Department of Agriculture," pp. 526, 529.

35. Theodore Roosevelt, "Forestry and Irrigation," p. 296; Pinchot, *The Fight for Conservation*, p. 27.

36. Pinchot, *The Fight for Conservation*, pp. 51-52; Gifford Pinchot, *A Primer of Forestry*, 2 vols. (Washington: U.S. Govt. Printing Office, 1899), 1: 65.

37. Pinchot, *The Fight for Conservation*, pp. 134, 137; McGee, "Scientific Work of the Department of Agriculture," p. 525; Bernhard E. Fernow, "The Practicability of an American Forest Administration," *Publications of the American Economic Association* 6, no. 3 (1891): 88; Pinchot, "Government Forestry Abroad," p. 9. See also Hays, *Conservation*, p. 271; and James Penick, Jr., *Progressive Politics and Conservation* (Chicago: Univ. of Chicago Press, 1968), pp. 16-17.

38. Hesmer, *Leben und Werk Von Dietrich Brandis*, pp. 370-71.

39. Richard C. Snyder and Glenn Paige, "The U.S. Decision to Resist Aggression in Korea," *Administrative Science Quarterly* 111, no. 3 (1958): 341-78. See also Gordon Bultena and John Hendee, "Forester Views of Interest Group Positions on Forest Policy," *Journal of Forestry* 70 (June 1972): 337-42. Gawthrop, *Bureaucratic Behavior*, p. 136.

40. Kaufman, *The Forest Ranger,* p. 207.

41. Robert K. Merton, "Bureaucratic Structure and Personality," *Social Forces* 18 (1940): 560-68. See also March and Simon, *Organizations,* pp. 37-40.

42. Kaufman, *The Forest Ranger,* p. 96.

43. William B. Devall, "The Forest Service and Its Clients: Input to Forest Service Decision-Making," *Environmental Affairs* 2 (Spring 1973): 752.

44. James D. Thompson, *Organizations in Action* (New York: McGraw-Hill, 1967), pp. 151-53.

45. Gawthrop, *Bureaucratic Behavior,* p. 181.

46. Thompson, *Organizations in Action,* p. 151. See also McNeil, "Understanding Organizational Power: Building on the Weberian Legacy," pp. 65-90.

Chapter 3

1. Ruby El Hult, *The Untamed Olympics* (Portland: Binford & Mort, 1954), pp. 56-57; S.A.D. Puter and Horace Stevens, *Looters of the Public Domain* (Portland: Portland Printing House, 1908), passim.

2. Gifford Pinchot, *Breaking New Ground* (New York: Harcourt, Brace, 1947), p. 321; McGeary, *Gifford Pinchot,* p. 80.

3. Hult, *The Untamed Olympics,* p. 214.

4. Ibid., pp. 173-78; Forest Supervisor P.S. Lovejoy to District Forester George Cecil, Dec. 22, 1911, in L Bdrys., Olympic, Box 53715, SEA.

5. District Chief of Operations C.H. Flory to Supervisor Fred Hansen, May 21, 1909, in L Bdrys., Box 53715, SEA. See the Antiquities Act of June 8, 1906, for explanation of this authority. The Biological Survey is now called the U.S. Fish and Wildlife Service.

6. Hult, *The Untamed Olympics,* p. 213.

7. Assistant Chief Forester C.S. Chapman to Cecil, Portland, July 28, 1909, in L Bdrys., Olympic, Box 53715, SEA.

8. Flory to Hansen, May 21, 1909, in L Bdrys., Olympic, Box 53715, SEA.

9. Chief of Biological Survey T.S. Palmer to Associate Chief Forester A.F. Potter, Sept. 13, 1910; Chief Forester Graves to Cecil, Oct. 6, 1910; Acting Chief Forester Leavitt to Cecil, Nov. 5, 1910: all in L Bdrys., Olympic, Box 53715, SEA.

10. Cecil to Graves, July 12, 1911, in L Bdrys., Olympic, Box 53715, SEA.

11. Cecil to "S staff," July 26, 1911; Cecil to Graves, July 31, 1911: both in L Bdrys., Olympic. Box 53715, SEA.

12. Lovejoy to Cecil, Aug. 17, 1911; Cecil to Graves, Aug. 30, 1911: both in L Bdrys., Olympic, Box 53715, SEA.

13. Lovejoy to Cecil, Nov. 9, 1911, in L Bdrys., Olympic, Box 53715, SEA.

14. Lovejoy to Cecil, Dec. 22, 1911, in L Bdrys., Olympic, Box 53715, SEA.

15. Associate Chief Forester Albert Potter to Cecil, Jan. 29, 1912; Lovejoy to Cecil, Feb. 17, 1912: both in L Bdrys., Olympic, Box 53715, SEA.

16. Assistant District Forester C.J. Buck to Graves, Feb. 26, 1912, in L Bdrys., Olympic, Box 53715, SEA.

17. Secretary of Agriculture D.F. Houston to Representative Albert Johnson, July 16, 1914; Assistant District Forester C.J. Buck to Supervisor R.L. Fromme, Aug. 4, 1914: both in L Bdrys., Olympic, Box 53715, SEA.

18. Fromme to Cecil, Aug. 7, 1914, in L Bdrys., Olympic, Box 53715, SEA.

19. Graves to "files," Dec. 3, 1914, in L Bdrys., Olympic, Box 53715, SEA.

20. Graves to Cecil, Dec. 3, 1914, in L Bdrys., Olympic, Box 53715, SEA.

21. Assistant Chief Forester W.B. Greeley to Graves, Apr. 1, 1915, in L Bdrys., Olympic, Box 53715, SEA. See also Horace M. Albright, "Statement to Committee on Public Lands," in U.S., Congress, House, Committee on Public Lands, *Hearings on H.R. 7086, The Proposed Mt. Olympus National Park,* 74th Congress, 2d sess., 1936, pp. 224-25.

22. Fromme to Cecil, Nov. 27, 1915; Graves to Cecil, Nov. 15, 1915; Fromme to district forester, July 23, 1915: all in L Bdrys., Olympic, Box 53715, SEA. Robert Shankland, *Steve Mather of the National Parks* (New York: Alfred A. Knopf, 1954), p. 78.

23. Albright, "Statement to Committee on Public Lands," pp. 224-25.

24. Fromme to Cecil, Nov. 27, 1915, in L Bdrys., Olympic, Box 53715, SEA.

25. See David Sucher, ed., *The Asahel Curtis Sampler* (Seattle: Puget Sound Access, 1973) for more about Curtis. For his later efforts Curtis has been memorialized by the Forest Service through a prominently marked picnic area and nature trail on Interstate Highway 5, just west of Snoqualmie Pass in Washington State.

26. Fromme to Cecil, Dec. 7, 1915, in L Bdrys., Olympic, Box 53715, SEA.

27. Graves successfully opposed this. See Graves to Representative William Kent, Jan. 31, 1916, in U.S., Congress, *Hearings on the Proposed Mount Olympus National Park,* p. 256.

28. Graves to Cecil, Jan. 12, 1916, in L Bdrys., Olympic, Box 53715, SEA.

29. Senate Clerk J. Ray Thompson to Secretary of Agriculture Houston, Mar. 30, 1916, in LP Bdrys., Olympic, WASO.

30. "Regional Working Plan for the Olympic Peninsula, Washington," parts 1 and 2, district 6, silviculture file copy, Mar. 18, 1916, in S Plans, Timber Mgmt. Policy Statements, 1915-1936, Box 59854, SEA.

31. Fromme to Cecil, June 20, 1916, in LP Bdrys., Olympic, WASO.

32. Fromme to Cecil, Aug. 29, 1916, in L Bdrys., Olympic, Box 53715, SEA.

33. Flory to Graves, Aug. 30, 1916, in L Bdrys., Olympic, Box 53715, SEA.

34. Fromme to Cecil, Sept. 2, 1916; Cecil to Graves, Sept. 11, 1916: both in L Bdrys., Olympic, Box 53715, SEA.

35. Houston to Representative A.F. Lever, Dec. 9, 1916, in L Bdrys., Olympic, WASO.

36. Graves to Palmer, Apr. 8, 1919, in Edward De Graaf, "The Olympic National Monument-National Forest-National Park," mimeographed summary of disposed-of files dealing with the Olympic elk in the Forest Service's Pacific Northwest Regional Office files, Feb. 1941, p. 4.

37. Gilligan, "The Development of Policy," pp. 74-75.

38. Buck to Fromme, June 11, 1921; Buck to "engineering," July 1, 1921: both in U Plans, Recreation, Olympic, Box 14683, SEA.

39. Assistant Chief Forester L.F. Kneipp to Cecil, May 1, 1922, in U Plans, Recreation, Olympic, Box 14683, SEA.

40. Board Resolution, Nov. 7, 1922; Fromme to M. Christy Thomas, Seattle Chamber of Commerce, Nov. 15, 1922; Kneipp to J.J. Underwood, Nov. 22, 1922; Fromme to Thomas B. Hill, Nov. 15, 1922; Buck to Fromme, Dec. 4, 1922: all in U Plans, Recreation, Olympic, Box 14683, SEA.

41. Fromme to Cecil, Feb. 4, 1921, in G Game, Cooperation, Box 99879, SEA; Resolution of the Clallam County Sportsmen's Assoc., Feb. 2, 1921, in De Graaf, "The Olympic National Monument," p. 5.

42. Fromme to Cecil, Dec. 14, 1921, in De Graaf, "The Olympic National Monument," p. 5.

43. *Port Angeles Evening News* clipping, Mar. 22, 1922, in De Graaf, "The Olympic National Monument," p. 5; *Congressional Record,* vol. 62, June 20, 1922, p. 13880; Hult, *The Untamed Olympics,* p. 217.

44. J.H. Billingslea, F.B. Myers, and R.L. Fromme, "Timber Management Plan, Olympic National Forest," in S Plans, Timber Mgmt., Box 59854, SEA.

45. United States Forest Service, district 6, *The Six-Twenty-Six,* vol. 9, no. 4, Apr. 1925, p. 1. Bound copies are in the Univ. of Washington Forestry Library, Seattle.

46. Ibid.

47. Ibid., pp. 19, 23.

48. Ibid., no. 5, May 1925, p. 16; no. 6, June 1925, pp. 23-24; no. 8, Aug. 1925, pp. 14-15.

49. *Congressional Record,* vol. 66, H.R. 13068, 69th Cong., 1926, p. 12017.

50. Assistant Solicitor M.F. Staley to Buck, Sept. 8, 1926, in LP Bdrys., Olympic, WASO.

51. Mathias to Folds, May 26, 1927, in LP Bdrys., Olympic, WASO.

52. Baldwin, "An Historical Study of the Wilderness Concept," p. 257; Gilligan, "The Development of Policy," pp. 130-31.

53. Acting Chief Forester C.M. Squire to Charles W. Folds, June 7, 1927, in LP Bdrys., Olympic, WASO.

54. Acting Chief Forester E.E. Carter to Senator W.L. Jones, June 2, 1927; Acting Secretary of Agriculture C.F. Marnin to Representative Johnson, June 8, 1927: both in LP Bdrys., Olympic, WASO.

55. Assistant District Forester E.N. Kavanagh to "lands," July 23, 1927, in LP Bdrys., Olympic, WASO.

56. Acting Assistant Chief Forester Robert R. Hill to District Forester C.M. Granger, Nov. 16, 1927, in LP Bdrys., Olympic, WASO.

57. See Kneipp to Representative Albert Johnson, Nov. 30, 9 1927, in LP Bdrys., Olympic, WASO.

58. F.W. Cleator to Dean Gordon D. Marckworth, chairman of the Olympic Park Review Committee, Sept. 10, 1953; copy is in possession of author.

59. Madison Grant to Park Service Director Stephen T. Mather, Oct. 22, 1928; Mather to Grant, Oct. 26, 1928; Acting Chief Forester Carter to Mather, Oct. 29, 1928: all in LP Bdrys., Olympic, WASO.

60. Greeley to Granger, Portland, Apr. 28, 1927, in S Plans, Timber Mgmt., Olympic, Box 54139, SEA.

61. Granger to "file," Apr. 16, 1929, in S Plans, Timber Mgmt., Shelton, Working Circle, Box 54139, SEA.

62. Granger to "file," Apr. 18, 1929; Chief Forester R.Y. Stuart to Granger, Apr. 26, 1929: both in S Plans, Timber Mgmt., Shelton, Working Circle, Box 54139, SEA.

63. Buck to "L file," June 19, 1929, in L Acquisition, Olympic, Box 53730, SEA.

64. Kneipp to Representative L.H. Hadley, Sept. 23, 1929, in LP Bdrys., Olympic, WASO.

65. Copy of report in D, Supervision, Meetings, Regional Foresters, 1935 and earlier, Box 21127, SEA.

66. Regional Forester C.J. Buck to lands and forest management staff, May 14, 1930, in LP Bdrys., Hood Canal Unit, Box 59809, SEA.

67. "Report on the Olympic Primitive Area," Nov. 5, 1930, in LP Bdrys., Hood Canal Unit, Box 59809, SEA.

68. Forest Supervisor H.L. Plumb to H.M. Myers of The Mountaineers, Jan. 19, 1931, in L Recreation, Olympic, Box 14686, SEA.

69. Gilligan, "The Development of Policy," pp. 289-90.

70. Willard Van Name, *Vanishing Forest Reserves* (Boston: Gorham Press, 1929), pp. 172-73. See also Fox, *John Muir and His Legacy,* pp. 174-82, 205.

71. See Kneipp to Buck, June 4, 1934, in L Bdrys., Olympic, WASO.

72. Kneipp to Washington office staff, Apr. 17, 1931, quoted in Gilligan, "The Development of Policy," pp. 141-43; ibid., pp. 143-45.

73. Park Service Director Albright to Stuart, June 16, 1931; Stuart to Albright, Oct. 1, 1931: both in L Bdrys., Umpqua, Diamond Lake, Box 40073, SEA. See also Arthur Maass, "Conservation, Political and Social Aspects," p. 272. This attempt to categorize and then apply expertise in the question without reference to lay authority is an example of the organization value of scientific elitism.

74. Stuart to Albright, Mar. 3, 1932, in L Bdrys., Umpqua, Diamond Lake, Box 40073, SEA; ibid., p. 12, emphasis added.

75. Record Group 95, "Minutes of the Service Committee," Aug. 18, 1932, p. 3.

76. Record Group 95, "Minutes of the Service Committee," Mar. 10, 1932; Richard Polenberg, *Reorganizing Roosevelt's Government* (Cambridge: Harvard Univ. Press, 1966), p. 5; Record Group 95, "Minutes of the Service Committee," Jan. 5, 1933.

77. Staff Forester F.E. Ames, Management Plan, Shelton Working Circle, Sept. 3, 1931, in S Plans, Timber Mgmt., Olympic, Box 54139, SEA.

78. Associate Chief Forester E.A. Sherman to H.E. Anthony, July 9, 1932, in De Graaf, "The Olympic National Monument," p. 6.

79. F.W. Mathias, resolutions to President Herbert Hoover, Nov. 7, 1932, copy in L Bdrys., Olympic, Box 53715, SEA.

80. Secretary of Agriculture Arthur M. Hyde to Mathias, Dec. 10, 1932; E.A. Goldman to Chief of the Biological Survey L. Redington, Nov. 16, 1932; Kavanagh to Stuart, Oct. 12, 1932: all in De Graaf, "The Olympic National Monument," pp. 7, 6, and 7, respectively.

81. Mathias to Anthony, Nov. 25, 1932, copy in L Bdrys., Olympic, Box 53715, SEA.

82. Plumb to Buck, Nov. 26, 1932; Assistant Regional Forester F.V. Horton to Plumb, Nov. 28, 1932: both in L Bdrys., Olympic, Box 53715, SEA.

83. Plumb to Mathias, Dec. 13, 1932, in L Bdrys., Olympic, Box 53715, SEA. The statements in this letter include the following organizational values: first, future scarcity of timber—hence the need to use land to the maximum efficiency; second, telic forestry—the desirability of national forest use to provide local community employment and production; and third, timber primacy—the idea that if the forest is managed for timber production, other goods and services will follow in sufficient amounts.

84. Record Group 95, "Minutes of the Service Committee," Jan. 5, 1933; U.S., Congress, Senate, Special Committee on Conservation of Wildlife Resources, vol. 421, 72nd Cong., Jan. 12-13, 1933, pp. 16-22, microfilm copy in Government Documents Div., Univ. of Washington Library, Seattle.

85. Stuart to Buck, Jan. 12, 1933; Anthony to Stuart, Jan. 17, 1933; Stuart to Anthony, Jan. 20, 1933: all in De Graaf, "The Olympic National Monument," pp. 7-8.

86. Assistant Chief Forester C.E. Rachford to T. Gilbert Pearson, Jan. 26, 1933; N.Y. Zoological Society to Stuart, Jan. 26, 1933: both in De Graaf, "The Olympic National Monument," p. 8.

87. Record Group 95, "Minutes of the Service Committee," Jan. 26, 1933.

88. *Port Angeles Evening News* Sept. 7, 1932, clipping in L Recreation, Olympic, Box 14686, SEA; Berry to Secretary of Agriculture Henry Wallace, Mar. 7, 1933; Kneipp to Berry, Mar. 13, 1933; Horton to Plumb, Mar. 22, 1933: all in LP Bdrys., Hood Canal Unit, 1939, Box 59809, SEA.

89. Buck to Rodney Glisan, president of the Mazamas, Apr. 10, 1933, copy to Plumb with added comments; Plumb to Buck, Apr. 11, 1933: both in LP Bdrys., Hood Canal Unit, 1939, Box 59809, SEA.

90. Buck to Roscoe Johnson, May 5, 1933, in LP Bdrys., Hood Canal Unit, 1939, Box 59809, SEA; The Mountaineers to Biological Survey, May 9, 1933, in De Graaf, "The Olympic National Monument," p. 8.

91. Polenberg, *Reorganizing Roosevelt's Government,* pp. 5-6, 8.

92. Kneipp to Buck, Aug. 29, 1933, in L Bdrys., Olympic, Confidential, Box 59809, SEA.

93. Gawthrop, *Bureaucratic Behavior in the Executive Branch,* p. 188.

94. Phillip Jacob and James Flink, "Values and Their Function in Decision-Making," *American Behavioral Scientist* 5 (May 1962): 25.

95. Marie Neal, *Values and Interests in Social Change* (Englewood Cliffs: Prentice Hall, 1965), p. 43.

96. Mortimer Smith, J.S. Bruner, and R.W. White, *Opinions and Personality* (New York: John Wiley, 1956), p. 277.

Chapter 4

1. Kneipp to Buck, Aug. 29, 1933; Plumb to Buck, Sept. 16, 1933; Buck to Plumb, Sept. 20, 1933: all in L Bdrys., Olympic, Confidential, Box 59809, SEA.

2. Buck to Stuart, Sept. 20, 1933, in L Bdrys., Olympic, Box 53715, SEA.

3. Record Group 95, "Minutes of the Service Committee," Sept. 28, 1933; Stuart to Buck, Oct. 18, 1933, in L Bdrys., Olympic, Box 53715, SEA.

4. Skinner to Anthony, Nov. 29, 1933 and May 3, 1934, in W Studies, Olympic Elk, Box 99879, SEA.

5. Horton to Kneipp, Nov. 1, 1933, handwritten, in LP Bdrys., Olympic, WASO.

6. Kneipp to Horton, Nov. 6, 1933, in L Bdrys., Olympic, Confidential, Box 59809, SEA.

7. Kneipp to Buck, Apr. 7, 1934, in L Bdrys., Olympic, Box 4341, SEA.

8. Steen, *The U.S. Forest Service,* pp. 196-97.

9. Ames to "Lands," Dec. 18, 1933, in L Bdrys., Olympic, Box 53715, SEA.

10. Staff Forester E.J. Hanzlik, Mar. 15, 1934, pp. 1 and 16, in S Plans, Timber Mgmt. Policy Statements, Box 59854, SEA.

11. Richard Polenberg, "Conservation and Reorganization: The Forest Service Lobby," *Agricultural History* 39 (1965): 230.

12. Ickes, *Secret Diary,* 2: 583.

13. Kneipp to Horton, Nov. 6, 1933, in L Bdrys., Olympic, Confidential, Box 59809, SEA.

14. Buck to Chief Forester Ferdinand Silcox, May 28, 1934, in L Bdrys., Olympic, Box 4341, SEA.

15. Kneipp to Buck, June 4, 1934, in L Bdrys., Olympic, WASO. See also Fox, *John Muir and His Legacy,* pp. 174-82.

16. Buck to Grays Harbor Chamber of Commerce (speech), May 22, 1934, in S Plans, Timber Mgmt., Olympic, Box 54139, SEA.

17. Rosalie Edge to D.H. Hanley, June 4, 1934; Hanley to George Drake, June 6, 1934; Plumb to Buck, June 13, 1934: all in L Bdrys., Olympic, Box 53715, SEA.

18. Supervisor of Rogue River National Forest to Buck, June 29, 1934; Plumb to Buck, June 25, 1934; O.A. Tomlinson to Plumb, June 16, 1934: all in L Bdrys., Olympic, Box 53715, SEA.

19. Plumb to Buck, June 18, 1934, in L Bdrys., Olympic, Box 53715, SEA.

20. Buck to Irving Clark, May 29, 1934, in L Recreation, Olympic, Box 14686, SEA.

21. Snoqualmie Forest Supervisor John Kuhns to Buck, June 27, 1934, in L Bdrys., Olympic, Box 53715, SEA.

22. Horton to Plumb, June 26, 1934, in L Bdrys., Olympic, Confidential, Box 59809, SEA.

23. Horton to Plumb, June 29, 1934, in L Bdrys., Olympic, Box 53715, SEA, and July 25, 1934, in L Bdrys., Olympic, Confidential, Box 59809, SEA.

24. Kavanagh to "Lands," Aug. 2, 1934, in L Bdrys., Olympic, Box 53715, SEA.

25. Horton to Plumb, July 5, 1934, in L Bdrys., Olympic, Box 53715, SEA.

26. Silcox to Ovid Butler, June 25, 1934, copy in L Bdrys., Olympic, Box 53715, SEA. Note the value of telic forestry expressed in Silcox's statement.

27. Assistant Regional Forester F.H. Brundage to Plumb, June 7, 1935, in S Plans, Timber Mgmt., Shelton Working Circle, Box 54139, SEA.

28. "Heintzleman Report," Mar. 17, 1936, in S Plans, Timber Mgmt., Olympic, General, Box 53715, SEA.

29. Plumb to Buck, July 5, 1934, in L Bdrys., Olympic, Box 53715, SEA.

30. Horton to Plumb, July 25, 1934, in L Bdrys., Olympic, Box 53715, SEA.

31. Horton to Kneipp, Aug. 14, 1934, handwritten, in LP Bdrys., Olympic, WASO.

32. Kneipp to Horton, July 9, 1934, in L Bdrys., Rogue River, Box 40073, SEA.

33. Kneipp to Buck, Portland, Aug. 21, 1934, in LP Bdrys., Olympic, Box 53715, SEA.

34. "Minutes of the State Planning Council," which quote H. L. Plumb's talk to their special committee about the Mount Olympus National Monument. Copy forwarded by Buck to Silcox, Aug. 31, 1934.

35. *Seattle Times,* Sept. 30, 1934. See Plumb to Buck, Oct. 2, 1934; Horton to Plumb, Oct. 8, 1934; Plumb to Horton (handwritten) Oct. 8, 1934: all in LP Bdrys., Olympic, Box 53715, SEA.

36. Buck to Silcox, Oct. 12, 1934; Kneipp to Buck, Dec. 1, 1934: both in LP Bdrys., Olympic, Box 53715, SEA.

37. Plumb to G.E. Munn, Jan. 5, 1935, in LP Bdrys., Olympic, Box 53715, SEA.

38. Report by E.J. Hanzlik, Jan. 28, 1935, in LP Bdrys., Olympic, WASO.

39. Preston Macy, George Grant, O.A. Tomlinson, and David Madsen to Park Service Director Arno Cammerer, Oct. 5, 1934; Buck to Silcox, Feb. 6, 1935: both in L Bdrys., Olympic, Box 53715, SEA.

40. Plumb to Buck, Feb. 28, 1935, copy in LP Bdrys., Olympic, WASO.

41. Horton to Kneipp, Mar. 13, 1935; Kneipp to Horton, Mar. 20, 1935: both in LP Bdrys., Olympic, WASO.

42. Kneipp to Buck, Feb. 14, 1935, in L Bdrys., Olympic, Box 53715, SEA.

43. Sherman to Smith, Apr. 3, 1935, in LP Bdrys., Olympic, WASO.

44. Buck to Silcox, Apr. 12, 1935, in LP Bdrys., Olympic, WASO.

45. Ibid.

46. Staff Forester I.J. Mason, "Grays Harbor Study," Apr. 4, 1935, in S Plans, Timber Mgmt., Olympic, 1927-1935, Box 54139, SEA.

47. Ibid., p. 8.

48. W.C. Mumaw to Buck, Oct. 14, 1935; Mumaw to Buck, Nov. 14, 1935: both in S Plans, Timber Mgmt., Olympic, 1927-1935, Box 54139, SEA.

49. Hanzlik to Forest Supervisor J.R. Bruckart, Nov. 2, 1935, in S Plans, Timber Mgmt., Olympic, 1927-1935, Box 54139, SEA.

50. T.T. Aldwell to Bruckart, Nov. 5, 1935, in S Plans, Timber Mgmt., Olympic, 1927-1935, Box 54139, SEA.

51. Buck to Mumaw, Nov. 20, 1935, in S Plans, Timber Mgmt., Olympic, 1927-1935, Box 54139, SEA.

52. Buck to Silcox, Jan. 31, 1936, in S Plans, Timber Mgmt., Olympic, 1927-1935, Box 54139, SEA.

53. B. Frank Heintzleman, "A Discussion of Measures to Help Stabilize the Grays Harbor Region," Mar. 17, 1936, in S Plans, Timber Mgmt., Olympic, General, 1936-1951, Box 54139, SEA.

54. Ibid.

55. See James Stevens, *Green Power: The Story of Public Law 273* (Seattle: Superior Publishing, 1958), passim.

56. O.J. Murie to Buck, Apr. 12, 1935, in De Graaf, "The Olympic National Monument," p. 19.

57. Brundage to Silcox, May 14, 1935; Buck to "Range Management," May 17, 1935; Buck to Silcox, July 1, 1935: all in W Studies, Olympic Elk, 1934-1935, Box 99879, SEA.

58. Plumb to "Lands," Jan. 28, 1936, in L Bdrys., Olympic, Confidential, Box 59809, SEA.

59. Quoted in Horton to Kneipp, June 11, 1935, handwritten, in LP Bdrys., Olympic, WASO.

60. Horton to Kneipp, June 10, 1935, handwritten, in LP Bdrys., Olympic, WASO.

61. Horton to Kneipp, July 6, 1935, handwritten, in LP Bdrys., Olympic, WASO.

62. Kneipp to Horton, July 12, 1935, in LP Bdrys., Olympic, WASO.

63. Polenberg, "Conservation and Reorganization," p. 230; Bruckart to Buck, Dec. 30, 1935, in L Bdrys., Olympic, Confidential, Box 59809, SEA.

64. Ibid.

65. Bruckart to District Ranger Olander, Jan. 25, 1936, in L Bdrys., Olympic, Confidential, Box 59809, SEA; retired Olympic National Forest staffer E. Loners to Ben W. Twight, Aug. 7, 1969.

66. Plumb to "Lands," Jan. 28, 1936, in L Bdrys., Olympic, Confidential, Box 59809, SEA.

67. President F.D. Roosevelt to secretaries of agriculture and interior, Feb. 18, 1936, in LP Bdrys., Olympic, WASO.

68. Carter to Granger, undated, in LP Bdrys., Olympic, WASO. Assistant

Chief Forester C.M. Granger had already made his own notes on suggested changes in the draft. A comment of Carter's across the bottom of his notes gives some feeling for the effort at collegial solidarity attempted by the chief forester's staff in its answer to the president: "C.M. G[ranger] says for me to discuss with Kneipp, including Granger's pencil notes, looking toward such modifications of the memo as will bring us all behind it."

69. Wallace to F.D. Roosevelt, Mar. 9, 1936, in LP Bdrys., Olympic, WASO. The draft was not sent.

70. Ibid.

71. Ibid.

72. Wallace to F.D. Roosevelt, Mar. 12, 1936, in LP Bdrys., Olympic, WASO. The draft was not sent.

73. Ibid.

74. Special Assistant Chief Forester R.F. Hammatt to "files," Mar. 18, 1936, in LP Bdrys., Olympic, WASO.

75. R.S. Yard to Silcox, Dec. 30, 1935, in LP Bdrys., Olympic, WASO.

76. This is not true. The monument creation was requested by the Biological Survey and Congressman Humphrey of Tacoma; it was opposed by the Forest Service law officer. See Acting District Forester C.H. Flory to Forest Supervisor Fred Hansen, May 21, 1909, in L Bdrys., Olympic, Mt. Olympus National Monument, 1905-1916, Box 53715, SEA.

77. Associate Chief Forester Earle Clapp to Yard, Mar. 24, 1936, in LP Bdrys., Olympic, WASO.

78. Ibid.

79. Yard to Silcox, Apr. 21, 1936, in LP Bdrys., Olympic, WASO.

80. "Report on the Olympic Primitive Area," Apr. 14, 1936, in LP Bdrys., Hood Canal Unit, 1939, Box 59809, SEA.

81. Staff Forester Fred Matz to "Timber Management," Apr. 2 and 3, 1936, in S Plans, Timber Mgmt., Olympic, Box 54139, SEA, and LP Bdrys., Hood Canal Unit, Box 59809, SEA; Horton to Bruckart, Apr. 10, 1936, in LP Bdrys., Hood Canal Unit, Box 59809, SEA.

82. Bruckart form letter, Sept. 15, 1936; Silcox to Wallace, June 29, 1936, copy; Kneipp to Buck, July 3, 1936: all in LP Bdrys., Olympic, Box 59809, SEA.

83. B. Frank Heintzleman, "Suggested Timber Management Plans, Olympic National Forest," June 30, 1936, in S Plans, Timber Mgmt., Olympic, Box 54139, SEA.

Chapter 5

1. Personal interview with Herbert L. Plumb, Aug. 9, 1969.

2. Kneipp to New York Herald Tribune, Apr. 6, 1936; Hammatt to Kneipp, Apr. 9, 1936: both in LP Bdrys., Olympic, WASO.

3. Buck to Hammatt, Apr. 16, 1936, in LP Bdrys., Olympic, Oly. Nat. Park, Box 40073, SEA; Horton to Bruckart, Apr. 17, 1936, in LP Bdrys., Hood Canal Unit, 1939, Box 59809, SEA.

4. See U.S., Congress, House, Committee on Public Lands, *Hearings on the Proposed Mount Olympus National Park,* 74th Cong., 2d sess., 1936, pp. 1-257 and passim.

5. Ibid., pp. 182-85.

6. Ibid., p. 193.

7. Ibid., pp. 197-98.

8. Ibid., p. 198.

9. Ibid., p. 257.

10. Kneipp to Silcox, June 4, 1936, in LP Bdrys., Olympic, WASO.

11. Silcox to Wallace, June 29, 1936, copy in LP Bdrys., Hood Canal Unit, 1939, Box 59809, SEA.

12. Plumb to "Lands files," June 8, 1936, in L Bdrys., Olympic, Confidential, Box 59809, SEA.

13. Hammatt to Brundage, Sept. 14, 1936, in LP Bdrys., Olympic, 1936, WASO.

14. Granger to Kneipp, Sept. 23, 1936, handwritten, in LP Bdrys., Olympic, WASO.

15. Hammatt to Washington office staff, Oct. 6, 1936, in LP Bdrys., Olympic, WASO.

16. Ibid.

17. Kneipp to Buck, Oct. 8, 1936, in LP Bdrys., Olympic, WASO.

18. Horton to Clapp, Oct. 14, 1936, handwritten, in LP Bdrys., Olympic, WASO. Frankland was regional engineer for the Forest Service. J.D. Ross was the superintendent of the Seattle City Lighting Department, which at that time was beginning construction of a large hydroelectric project on national forest lands northeast of Seattle.

19. Kneipp to Horton, Oct. 22, 1936, in LP Bdrys., Olympic, WASO.

20. Kneipp to Buck, Oct. 8, 1936, in L Bdrys., Olympic, WASO.

21. Kneipp to Horton, Nov. 2, 1936, in LP Bdrys., Olympic, 1936-1951, Box 40073, SEA.

22. Range Examiner John Schwartz to Buck, Nov. 16, 1936, in De Graaf, "The Olympic National Monument," p. 21.

23. Bruckart to Buck, Dec. 3, 1936, in De Graaf, "The Olympic National Monument," p. 22.

24. Kneipp to Granger, Dec. 9, 1936, in LP Bdrys., Olympic, WASO.

25. Kneipp to Hammatt, Dec. 17, 1936, in LP Bdrys., Olympic, WASO.

26. Kneipp to Buck, Dec. 21, 1936, in LP Bdrys., Olympic, WASO.

27. H.S. Graves to Herbert A. Smith, Dec. 29, 1936, in LP Bdrys., Olympic, WASO.

28. Kneipp to Buck, Jan. 13, 1937, in LP Bdrys., Olympic, WASO.

29. Buck to Silcox, Jan. 23, 1937, in LP Bdrys., Olympic, WASO.

30. Kneipp to chief forester's staff, Jan. 26, 1937; Silcox to Wallace, Feb. 12, 1937: both in LP Bdrys., Olympic, WASO.

31. Kneipp to Horton, Feb. 12, 1937, in LP Bdrys., Olympic, WASO.

32. Kneipp to Buck, Feb. 18, 1937, in LP Bdrys., Olympic, WASO.

33. Fromme to Horton, Feb. 5, 1937; Fromme to Horton, Feb. 6, 1937: both in L Bdrys., Olympic, Confidential, Box 59809, SEA; Bruckart to Buck, Feb. 17, 1937, in L Bdrys., Mt. Olympus N.M., 1938, Box 59809, SEA.

34. Horton to Kneipp, Feb. 23, 1937, handwritten, in LP Bdrys., Olympic, WASO.

35. Region Six's suggested Timber Statement on H.R. 4724, Feb. 23, 1937, in LP Bdrys., Olympic, WASO. There are some interesting adjuncts to the enumerated items of the timber statement summary. The second item shows that the massive development of the Boeing Company and other technological industries was obviously not foreseen. The estimated pulp figures in item four not only assumed stable future markets, prices, and technology, but also assumed no influence of essentially uncut stands on national forest lands. It was based on a rotation for pulpwood of seventy years (Hoffman to "forest management," June 5, 1935, in S Plans, Timber Mgmt., Olympic, Box 54139, SEA), though rotations of forty to fifty years could have been used since volume increment rates of western hemlock diminish after thirty years. See David R.M. Scott, "The Pacific Northwest Region," in *Regional Silviculture of the United States*, ed. John Barrett (New York: Ronald Press, 1962), pp. 548-49. The importance of item five was dismissed when the park was created and there was still plenty of timber *and* Grays Harbor became a large export port for logs (for example, in 1969 Aberdeen was the leading log exporting port, with 393 million board feet of logs being exported). See John W. Austin, *Production, Prices, Employment, and Trade (Portland: U.S. Forest Service, PNW For. Exp. Sta., 1969), p. 9.*

36. Horton to Kneipp, Mar. 6, 1937, two handwritten letters, in LP Bdrys., Olympic, WASO.

37. Silcox to R.K. Tiffany, Mar. 9, 1937, in LP Bdrys., Olympic, WASO.

38. B.H. Kizer to Silcox, Mar. 12, 1937, in LP Bdrys., Olympic, WASO.

39. Assistant Secretary of Agriculture James D. LeCron to Irving Brant, Apr. 10, 1937, in LP Bdrys., Olympic, WASO.

40. Brant to Wallace, Apr. 24, 1937, in LP Bdrys., Olympic, WASO.

41. Clapp to Kneipp, June 7, 1937, in LP Bdrys., Olympic, WASO.

42. Gilligan, "The Development of Policy," pp. 174-203.

43. Robert Marshall to chief forester's staff, undated (though about Apr. 24, 1937), in LP Bdrys., Olympic, WASO.

44. Rachford to Clapp, Apr. 25, 1937, handwritten, in LP Bdrys., Olympic, WASO.

45. Gilligan, "The Development of Policy," pp. 189-91. See also, Fox, *John Muir and His Legacy,* p. 206 and passim; and Nash, *Wilderness,* pp. 206-7.

46. Clapp to Kneipp, June 7, 1937, in LP Bdrys., Olympic, WASO.

47. Hammatt to Silcox, Apr. 26, 1937, in LP Bdrys., Olympic, WASO.

48. Draft of proposed letter from Wallace to Public Lands Committee Chairman Rene De Rouen, June 9, 1937, in LP Bdrys., Olympic, WASO.

49. Kneipp to Greeley, June 29, 1937, in LP Bdrys., Olympic, WASO.

50. Buck to Silcox, July 17, 1937; Assistant Chief Forester Granger to Buck, July 26, 1937: both in LP Bdrys., Olympic, WASO.

51. Granger to Buck, July 30, 1937, in LP Bdrys., Olympic N.P., Box 40073, SEA.

52. Wallace to De Rouen, Aug. 13, 1937, in LP Bdrys., Olympic, WASO; also found in S Plans, Timber Mgmt., Olympic, Mt. Oly. N. M., Box 54139, SEA.

53. Buck to Clapp, Aug. 28, 1937, copy in D Supervision, Presidential Trip in R-6, 1937, Box 21127, SEA.

54. Buck to Silcox, Sept. 2, 1937, in D Supervision, Presidential Trip in R-6, 1937, Box 21127, SEA.

55. Buck to Silcox, Sept. 29, 1937; Assistant Chief Forester Earl Loveridge to Buck, Sept. 30, 1937: telegram copies of both in D Supervision, Presidential Trip in R-6, 1937, Box 21127, SEA (also found in LP Bdrys., Olympic, WASO).

56. Gilligan, "The Development of Policy," p. 166.

57. Bruckart to "files," Oct. 6, 1937, in LP Bdrys., Olympic, WASO. Receipt date not noted.

58. Personal interview with Plumb, Aug. 9, 1969.

59. District Ranger L.D. Blodgett to Bruckart, Oct. 22, 1937, in L Bdrys., Olympic, Confidential, Box 59809, SEA.

60. Bruckart to Buck, Oct. 25, 1937, copy in L Bdrys., Olympic, WASO.

61. Buck to Silcox, Oct. 29, 1937, in L Bdrys., Olympic, WASO.

62. Kneipp to Granger, Silcox, Clapp, and staff, Nov. 2, 1937, in L Bdrys., Olympic, WASO.

63. Kneipp to Granger, Clapp, Silcox, and staff, Nov. 1, 1937, in L Bdrys., Olympic, WASO.

64. Silcox to Kneipp, Nov. 18, 1937, in L Bdrys., Olympic, WASO; Buck to Silcox, Nov. 4, 1937, in De Graaf, "The Olympic National Monument," p. 24; Hult, *The Untamed Olympics,* p. 219.

65. Granger to all regions, Jan. 10, 1938, in LP Bdrys., Olympic N.P., 1936-1951, Box 40073, SEA.

66. Buck to Silcox, Jan. 21, 1938, in LP Bdrys., Olympic, WASO.

67. Assistant Secretary of Agriculture Paul Appleby to Silcox, Jan. 14, 1938, in LP Bdrys., Olympic, WASO.

68. Granger to "C Legislation," Jan. 21, 1938, in LP Bdrys., Olympic, WASO.

69. Buck to Silcox, Jan. 21, 1938, in LP Bdrys., Olympic, WASO.

70. Buck to Brundage, Jan. 25, 1938, in L Bdrys., Olympic, 1938, Proposed Olympic Forest Wilderness, Box 53715, SEA.

71. Clapp to Silcox, Jan. 28, 1938; Carter to Granger, Jan. 22, 1938, handwritten: both in LP Bdrys., Olympic, WASO.

72. Brundage to Buck, Feb. 1, 1938, in L Bdrys., Olympic, 1938, Proposed Olympic Forest Wilderness, Box 53715, SEA.

73. Silcox to Appleby, Feb. 15, 1938, in LP Bdrys., Olympic, WASO.

74. Quoted in Bruckart to Buck, Feb. 3, 1938, in L Bdrys., Olympic, 1938, Proposed Olympic Forest Wilderness, Box 53715, SEA.

75. Buck to Brundage, Feb. 15, 1938, in L Bdrys., Mt. Olympus N. M., Box 59809, SEA.

76. Brundage to Bruckart, Feb. 23, 1938, in L Bdrys., Mt. Olympus N.M., Box 59809, SEA.

77. Silcox to Appleby, Feb. 15, 1938, in LP Bdrys., Olympic, WASO.

78. Other aspects of the controversy over the Olympic National Park and the history of the Olympic forest can be followed in the following references: Elmo Richardson, "Olympic National Park, 20 Years of Controversy," *Forest History* 12 (Jan. 1969): 6-15; Carsten Lien, "The Olympic Boundary Struggle," *The Mountaineer* 52 (Apr. 1959): 18-35; Hult, *The Untamed Olympics,* passim; Edwin Van Syckle, *They Tried to Cut It All* (Seattle: Pacific Search Press, 1980), passim.

Chapter 6

1. Hays, *Conservation,* pp. 190-98.

2. McConnell, *Private Power,* p. 360.

3. Kaufman, *The Forest Ranger,* passim; Schiff, "Innovation and Administrative Decision-Making," p. 5.

4. Fremont J. Lyden, "Using Parsons' Functional Analysis in the Study of Public Organizations," *Administrative Science Quarterly* 20 (Mar. 1975): 66-67.

5. R.W. Behan, "The Succotash Syndrome, or Multiple Use: A Heartfelt Approach to Forest Land Management," *Natural Resources Journal* 7 (1967): 473-78; Polenberg, "Conservation and Reorganization," p. 231.

6. Hays, *Conservation,* p. 271; Maass, "Conservation, Political and Social Aspects," p. 276.

7. The Grand Teton controversy is thoroughly covered from the Park Service perspective by Donald Swain, *Wilderness Defender: Horace M. Albright and Conservation* (Chicago: Univ. of Chicago Press, 1970), pp. 113-29 and 252-86; C. J. Olsen, assistant regional forester, Ogden, Utah, to Horton, Oct. 24, 1936, in L Bdrys., Olympic, confidential, Box 59809, SEA; Swain, *Wilderness Defender,* p. 263.

8. Stuart to Albright, Mar. 3, 1932, p. 5, copy in L Bdrys., Rogue River, Crater Lake National Park, Box 40073, SEA; Gilligan, "The Development of Policy," p. 166.

9. Alan R. Sommarstrom, "Wildland Preservation Crisis: The North Cascades Controversy" (Ph.D. diss., Univ. of Washington, 1970), passim.

10. Stuart to Albright, Mar. 3, 1932; Gilligan, "The Development of Policy," p. 159.

11. Parsons, "General Theory in Sociology," 1: 10-16.

12. Thompson, *Organizations in Action,* p. 11.

13. Parsons, "General Theory in Sociology," 1: 16; idem, *The Social System* (Glencoe, Ill.: Free Press, 1951), pp. 376-77.

14. W. Keith Warner and Eugene Havens, "Goal Displacement and the Intangibility of Organizational Goals," *Administrative Science Quarterly* 13 (1968): 541; George A. Shipman, "Complexities of Goal Attainment," *Public Administration Review* 29 (1969): 211.

15. Donal V. Allison, "The Development and Use of Political Power of Federal Agencies: A Case Study of the U.S. Forest Service" (Master's thesis, Univ. of Virginia, 1965), pp. 77-78.

16. Thompson, *Organizations in Action,* p. 153; this analysis is based on Parsons, "General Theory in Sociology," 1: 16-20; and Parsons and Neil Smelser, *Economy and Society* (New York: Free Press, 1956), pp. 49, 56.

Appendix

The Theoretical Nature of Values

Contrary to the economic use of the term "value," the sociological use of the term does not usually refer to a measure of material wealth. Value indicates a normative standard that persists over time; in other words, it is a standard or code that exerts a normative (controlling) influence on human behavior. Kluckhohn has defined value as "a *conception,* explicit or implicit, distinctive of an individual or characteristic of a group, of the desirable which influences the selection from available models, means, and ends of action.";1

William R. Catton refines this definition by stating that "a value is a conception of the desirable which is implied by a set of preferential responses to symbolic desiderata."[2] A value is not just a preference; it is considered to be the proper set of choices, justified morally, rationally, or aesthetically, or in combination. Valuing behavior exhibits regularity, a relatively stable pattern of choice repeatedly observable over time, so that an inductive inference can be made that the choice is typical.

"Value orientation" is a "definition of the situation," a group's perception of what in fact is, what ought to be, and what must be done. The term involves both value elements and existential premises, or what human beings consider to be facts. Kluckhohn has formally defined value orientation as "a generalized and organized conception, influencing behavior, of nature, of man's place in it, of man's relation to man, and of the desirable and nondesirable as they may relate to man-environment and interhuman relations."[3]

The Function of Value Orientation

Organizations such as public bureaucracies are social systems that are characterized by roles, norms, and values. Roles serve to differentiate among the members of the organization, whereas norms and values integrate the members. Norms make explicit the expected behavior of the organization; values and value orientation furnish the more complex and broad justification both for appropriate behavior and for the tasks and outputs of the organization. They include the ruling or sanctioned patterns that prescribe the organizationally approved ways of doing things and the established goals of the organizational system or subculture. Katz and Kahn point out that these group values are the standards to which reference is made for judging acceptable and unacceptable behavior of relevance to the system.[4]

Value orientation contributes to the selection and emphasis of certain perceptions or images in preference to others. It also erects barriers against images and perceptions conflicting with or threatening to the organization's values. Bruner, Postman, and McGinnies state that "value orientation makes for *perceptual sensitization* to value stimuli, leads to *perceptual defense* against inimical stimuli, and gives rise to a process of *value resonance* which keeps the person responding in terms of objects valuable to him even when such objects are absent from his immediate environment."[5]

Value orientation can also be described as a cultural retention mechanism in organizations. The basic beliefs and values of the organization are retained by passing them on to the new members through institutionalization. Aldrich observes that such retention is facilitated in organizations which have achieved some degree of insulation from environmental pressures, which maintain strong internal selection pressures that are biased toward standardization, and which root out deviance and exert strong pressures toward uniformity of outlook. Continuity in leadership helps to preserve such patterns.[6]

Apparently, value orientation is an important influence on the behavior of members of a public agency because it not only guides the way an organization perceives its mission or purpose in society, but it also filters the agency's perception of public demands. Furthermore, public agencies often reinforce particular value orientations through both organizational and professional loyalty and identity-building, sometimes termed "esprit de corps."[7]

Notes

1. Clyde Kluckhohn, "Values and Value Orientations in the Theory of Action: An Exploration in Definition and Classification," in *Toward A General Theory of Action,* ed. Talcott Parsons and Edward A. Shils (New York:

Harper Torchbooks, 1962), p. 395; emphasis added. For a broad discussion of this and other ways of defining values, see Richard N.L. Andrews and Mary J. Watts, "Theory and Methods of Environmental Values Research," *Interdisciplinary Science Review* 5 (Mar. 1980): 71-78. For a recent study using Kluckhohn's value orientation concept, see Mark Iutcovich, "Time Perception: A Case Study of a Developing Nation," *Sociological Focus* 12 (1979): 71-85.

2. William R. Catton, Jr., *From Animistic to Naturalistic Sociology* (New York: McGraw-Hill, 1966), pp. 130-33.

3. Kluckhohn, "Values and Value Orientations," p. 411.

4. Katz and Kahn, *The Social Psychology of Organizations,* pp. 385-86.

5. Jerome Bruner, Leo Postman, and Elliot McGinnies, "Personal Values as Selective Factors in Perception," *Journal of Abnormal and Social Psychology* 43 (1948): 142-54; emphasis added. A more recent study also confirms that values determine priorities. See G. David Hughes, V.R. Rao, and H.A. Akler, "The Influences of Values, Information, and Decision Orders on a Public Policy Decision," *Journal of Applied Social Psychology* 6, no. 2 (1976): 145-58.

6. Howard E. Aldrich, *Organizations and Environments* (Englewood Cliffs: Prentice Hall, 1979), pp. 46-51.

7. Katz and Kahn, *The Social Psychology of Organizations,* p. 363.